Michael Faraday

Physics and Faith

OXFORD
PORTRAITS
IN SCIENCE

Owen Gingerich
General Editor

Michael Faraday

Physics and Faith

Colin A. Russell

Oxford University Press

To Josiah, Harriet, and Emma

OXFORD
UNIVERSITY PRESS

Oxford   New York
Athens   Auckland   Bangkok   Bogotá   Buenos Aires   Calcutta
Cape Town   Chennai   Dar es Salaam   Delhi   Florence   Hong Kong   Istanbul
Karachi   Kuala Lumpur   Madrid   Melbourne   Mexico City   Mumbai
Nairobi   Paris   São Paulo   Singapore   Taipei   Tokyo   Toronto   Warsaw
and associated companies in
Berlin   Ibadan

Copyright © 2000 by Colin A. Russell
Published by Oxford University Press, Inc.
198 Madison Avenue, New York, New York   10016
www.oup.com

Design: Design Oasis
Layout: Leonard Levitsky
Picture research: Colin A. Russell and Amla Sanghvi

Library of Congress Cataloging-in-Publication Data
Russell, Colin Archibald.
Michael Faraday: physics and faith / Colin A. Russell.
p. cm. – (Oxford portraits in science)
Includes bibliographical references and index.
Summary: A biography of the nineteenth-century English scientist whose religious beliefs
guided his exploration of electricity and magnetism.
ISBN 0-19-511763-8 (lib.)
1. Faraday, Michael, 1791–1867—Juvenile literature. 2. Physicists—Great Britain—
Biography—Juvenile literature. [1. Faraday, Michael, 1791–1867. 2. Physicists.]
I. Title. II. Series.
QC16.F2.R87 2000
530'.092—dc21
[B]   00-027008

9 8 7 6 5 4 3 2 1
Printed in the United States of America
on acid-free paper

Cover: *Michael Faraday in later life;* inset: *a portrait by Charles Turner.*
Frontispiece: *Faraday in middle age.*

Contents

OXFORD PORTRAITS IN SCIENCE

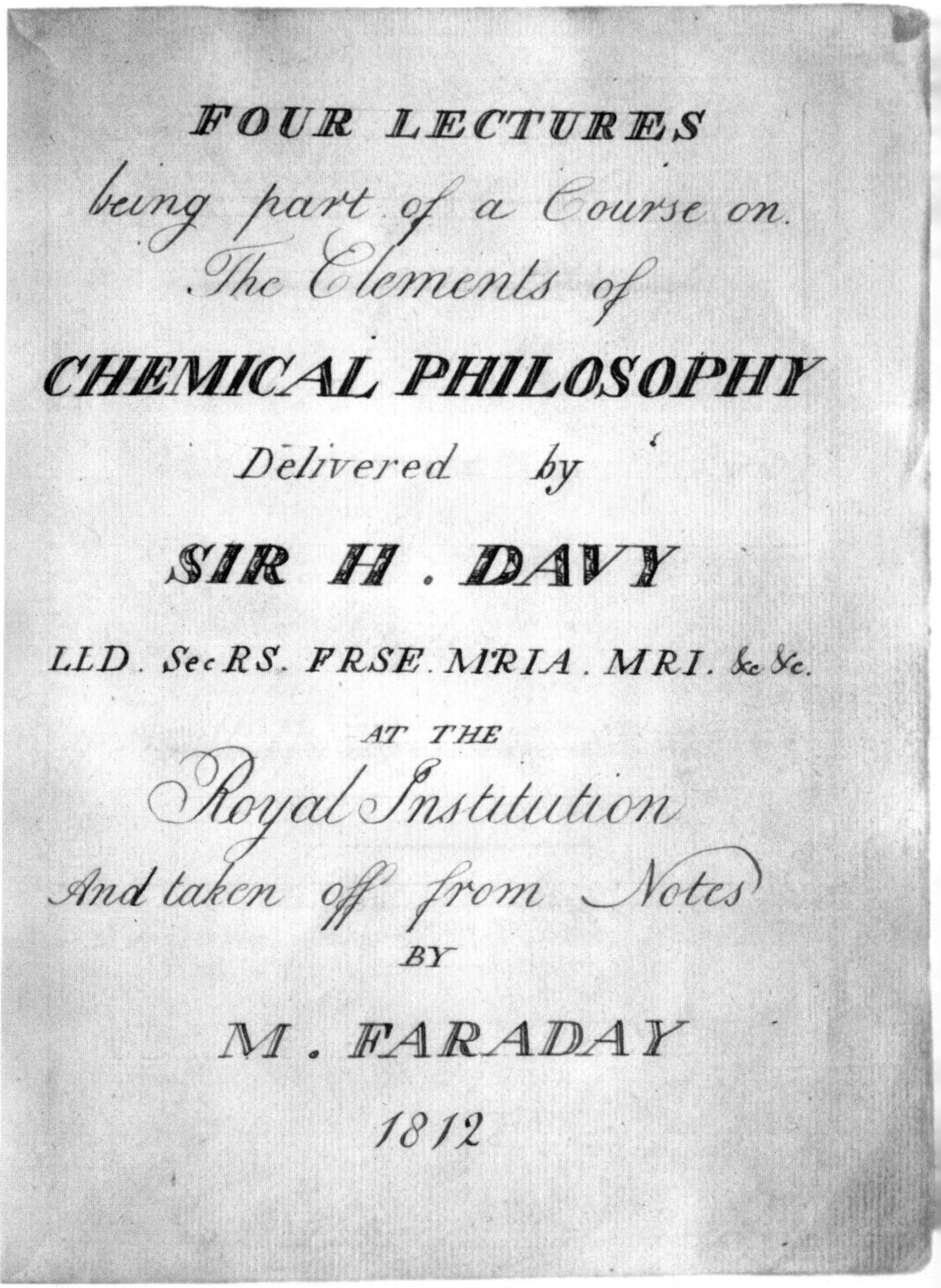

FOUR LECTURES

being part of a Course on

The Elements of

CHEMICAL PHILOSOPHY

Delivered   by

SIR H . DAVY

LLD . Sec RS . FRSE . MRIA . MRI . &c &c.

AT THE

Royal Institution

And taken off from Notes

BY

M . FARADAY

1812

The title page of Michael Faraday's notes on a course of chemical lectures by Sir Humphry Davy, which Faraday attended in 1812. By great good fortune no one ever discarded his original notes.

The Theater of Science

One evening in February 1812 crowds were gathering in a street in the heart of London's West End. The focus of their interest was 21 Albemarle Street, the home of what is properly called the Royal Institution of Great Britain. Soon, however, the warmth inside beckoned them in from the chilly night. Carriages jostled for position near the front doors, and such was the pressure of horse-drawn traffic that the authorities had imposed the unprecedented restriction of making it a one-way street, possibly the first in the world. As is the case today, traffic was allowed to move only from south to north from Piccadilly. Men and women, and perhaps even a few children, filed into the entrance hall and upstairs to the object of their pilgrimage. This was the great semicircular Lecture Theatre, its row after row of green seating accommodating up to 900 people and affording from every position a perfect view of the lecture table, on which an assortment of wonderful scientific apparatuses was already displayed. The buzz of excitement mounted as the moment approached for the doors behind the table to open and the lecturer to emerge. Meanwhile most of the audience would be at least equally interested in the fashions and deportment of each other, for this was in every sense a social occasion, where one was to see and be seen. Every year the lists of subscribers or members included titled persons, and even royal patrons might sometimes be observed in the front row. However, there was more serious business on hand.

They were to hear a lecture from one of London's favorite orators, only it was not about politics but science that he was to speak. His name was Humphry Davy, a young man who 11 years prior, in 1801, had electrified audiences with his accounts of what modern science was doing and what it surely could do in the future. By 1812 his fame was even greater. To attend a Davy Discourse at the Royal Institution was almost as fashionable an activity as the races at Epsom or a Garden Party at Buckingham Palace. You did not have to be a scientist to gain admittance. You could even be a poet. Davy was a friend of William Wordsworth and Samuel Taylor Coleridge, and wrote verse himself and shared their reverence for nature. Coleridge attended his lectures "to renew my stock of metaphors," and not a few of the ladies felt those sparkling eyes were designed for something better than gazing into crucibles.

This, then, was the lecturer appointed for the night of February 29, 1812. His address was on "Radiant Matter," the first of four lectures that completed a longer course on chemistry that Davy had begun the previous year. As always his lecture was received with rapturous applause, and the elite of London society dispersed to their next social function (probably dinner) while the rest melted away into the winter night. In fact, the evening's performance had been far removed from one of the original intentions of the founders of the Royal Institution (to promote agricultural chemistry), and one might be forgiven for supposing that the workers and artisans had been systematically elbowed out. In the original building, a separate staircase led directly from the street to a gallery included for the use of artisans. But such instruction of the lower classes was frowned upon and, at considerable expense, the staircase was soon pulled down. It was a symbolic gesture and for many decades the Royal Institution had the doubtful distinction of catering only to the rich and powerful.

Yet that night, high up in the topmost gallery, sitting right under the clock and far removed from his elders and betters, was a young man from a poor family who, by an astonishing piece of good fortune, had secured tickets for these last four lectures by Humphry Davy. He had to enter by the main doors, but it is doubtful if he was much noticed as, alone, he climbed up to his lofty seat. His name was quite unknown to any there: Michael Faraday. Once Davy had begun his lecture the young man had no thoughts of his own obscurity or of anything but the subject at hand, and, as was his habit, he took copious notes. When all was over he slipped away unnoticed, and, as he had done with other lectures, he wrote them up in great detail in the days that followed.

It may be that by the fourth lecture, a few of the regulars had become aware of the solitary figure beneath the clock. None of them, however, could have had the remotest idea that in fewer than 20 years, that same lecture theater would be filled to overflowing by audiences just as eager to hear Michael Faraday. His technique in demonstration experiments, like that of his predecessor, was superb, as were his enthusiasm and ability to communicate. Only now there were many differences. Fashion, though still present, was no longer the dominant note of the occasion. Young people attended in increasing numbers, and were even specially provided for in children's lectures. What Faraday may have lacked in poetic finesse compared to Davy was more than compensated for by a puckish sense of humor and goodwill. By the age of 40, he had become a scientist of international repute, having made fundamental discoveries not only in chemistry but also in electricity and magnetism. Through Faraday's work had come the invention of the electric motor and the dynamo. Faraday, like Davy before him, was to make the Royal Institution into one of the palaces of science. Here came fame and renown to a fortunate few, with scientific discoveries of such fundamental importance that it has been said that no other square mile anywhere in the world has witnessed such progress in science. Here also multitudes of ordinary men and women discovered a whole new world of experience—the world of the newly burgeoning sciences.

While Davy was building up a reputation for himself and the Royal Institution, he also found time for chemical research, which turned out to be of fundamental importance. Perhaps his major feat was to unite chemistry and electricity in electrochemistry, a new science on the border between classical chemistry and physics. In electrochemistry, chemical substances were subjected to the action of an electric current, and the very forces holding the particles of a compound body together were conceived as a kind of electrical attraction. The practical outcome was the isolation of a range of new, reactive, and exciting metals, including sodium, potassium, calcium, barium, and strontium. By 1812 Davy had become Joint Secretary of the Royal Society, had delivered no fewer than five of its prestigious Bakerian Lectures, and had received its Copley Medal. In fact he was also to gain the honor of a knighthood in April, two days before his final lecture and five days before his marriage to a rich widow.

Yet, in a curious sense, it may be said that at that lecture in 1812 Humphry Davy had unknowingly set in motion events that were to lead to revelations even more remarkable than he had seen in his laboratory, to lead to an acquaintanceship of immense power for science. Humphry Davy's greatest discovery, in the opinion of many observers, was in fact Michael Faraday.

This young man was soon to begin a career in science of such dazzling brilliance that he became a legend even in his

A KEEN MIND

Faraday's mind was so agile, and his thought so intense, that it is often hard for us to keep up with him. Frequently he was thinking about several topics at once. Any one week in his life might include chemical analysis, electric research, industrial consulting, and public presentations. His enthusiasm at the age of 19, as displayed in this excerpt from a letter to his friend Benjamin Abbott, would stay with him throughout his career.

My mind was deeply engaged on this subject, and was proceeding to place itself as fast as possible in the midst of confusion, when it was suddenly called to take care of the body by a very cordial, affectionate & also effectual salute from a spout. This of course gave a new turn to my ideas and from thence to Blackfriars Bridge it was busily bothered amongst Projectiles and Parabolas. At the Bridge the wind came in my face and directed my attention as well as earnestly as it could go to the inclination of the Pavement. Inclined Planes were then all the go and a further illustration of this point took place on the other side of the Bridge, where I happened to proceed in a very smooth, soft, and equable manner for the space of three or four feet. This movement, which is vulgarly called slipping, introduced the subject of friction, and the best method of lessening it, and in this frame of mind I went on with little or no interruption for some time except occasional and actual experiments connected with the subject in hand, or rather in head.

own time. In addition, there would be much serious thought about his Christian faith and a range of church activities, to say nothing of his life at home and delighted encounters with younger members of his extended family. To sum up his life is not easy, but from our distant standpoint it can be convincingly argued that Michael Faraday stands among the three or four greatest experimental scientists of all time.

Paul's Alley Meetinghouse in London was the home of the local congregation of Sandemanian Christians. Michael Faraday attended for many years and eventually became one of its leaders.

Faraday's Roots

The family roots of the Faradays may be traced to an area of England from which many of the great names of British science came in the first half of the 19th century. It was not Oxford or Cambridge—and certainly neither was it London—but it was rather that portion of England that encompasses the most northerly parts of Lancashire, the old county of Westmorland, and the northwest of Yorkshire. It is a wild, desolate area, with the Pennines to the east and the Cumbrian mountains to the northwest. The only towns of any size even today are Lancaster, Kendal, Sedbergh, and Kirkby Stephen. Yet from such an unpromising cradle emerged geologist Adam Sedgwick, chemists John Dalton and Edward Frankland, electrical-science pioneer William Sturgeon, anatomists William Turner and Richard Owen, engineers James Mansergh and Robert Rawlinson, and mathematician and philosopher William Whewell who became Master of Trinity College at Cambridge University.

These men of science, as well as many others, have been called "the hard progeny of the North," and it seems that the inhospitable climate and the rough terrain must have been one factor in promoting a certain toughness of mind that is so necessary in the pursuit of science. Also there was a sturdy independence of opinion in these remote areas so far away from London. And almost on their doorsteps were spectacular natural phenomena such as mountains, waterfalls, and caves, as well as abundant wildlife. These are known to have encouraged many a young person to explore the secrets of nature more deeply.

Although he was not born in this area, Michael Faraday knew that in these places lay his family roots for many generations. In fact his birth took place only a few weeks after the family had torn up their ancestral roots and settled in London. Up to that time his parents had lived in a place so remote and insignificant that none of their new metropolitan neighbors would even have heard of it. It lay in wild country near the border between two northern English counties, Yorkshire and Westmorland. Its name was Outhgill.

Imagine two ridges of high hills going roughly north-south, known on the east side as Mallerstang Fells and on the west as the Howgills. Between them is a remote valley that, in its higher reaches, gives birth to the River Eden, flowing north and destined after many miles to enter the great border city of Carlisle, finally reaching the sea in the Solway Firth. Apart from the occasional farmstead this mountainous country is still largely uninhabited. Since the 1870s the Eden has shared part of its valley with the famous Settle-Carlisle railway line, though today few trains disturb the peace of a countryside that is idyllic in summer and awesome in winter. The Mallerstang Fells loom majestically to the east, and from a train to Carlisle it is possible to get a glimpse at their foot of a few scattered buildings. Within a few seconds the train enters a tunnel and they are gone. But this tiny cluster of buildings was the home of the Faraday family, the hamlet of Outhgill.

Outhgill lies in an area steeped in history. A mile to the north lies the dramatic ruin known as Pendragon Castle, allegedly once the home of Uther, father of King Arthur.

Still farther back in history, the very border between England and Scotland once passed within a mile or two of Outhgill. In the days of the Faradays the only communication was a track from the small market town of Kirkby Stephen, five miles to the north, crossing the fells to the dales in the south, entering Yorkshire at Hell Gill Bridge. Even this lonely path was a few hundred yards west of the hamlet. This was the old drove road from Scotland along which cattle were driven to places as far away as London, 300 miles to the south. Along this track there also came horses in surprising numbers, some with passengers and others pulling heavy loads from the nearby lead mines which were, in those days, a hive of activity. Others were on their way to the great September fair just north of Kirkby Stephen. It was these horses that provided James Faraday, Michael's father, with his livelihood: he was a blacksmith.

Across the valley from Outhgill lay Deep Gill Farm, where Margaret Hastwell was a maidservant. Margaret was the younger sister of Mary Faraday, the bride of James's brother Richard. James would have known Margaret through visiting his brother and sister-in-law and perhaps through going to chapel. In 1786, nine years after the first Faraday-Hastwell union, there was another marriage, and Margaret became the wife of James Faraday. Their first two children, Elizabeth and Robert, were born in Outhgill.

Margaret Hastwell, Michael's mother, was a maidservant at this farmhouse in Mallerstang.

There can be little doubt that life in these parts was tough and grim at any time, though these were particularly difficult times. Family expectations and attitudes would be molded by such circumstances for more than just the current generation. Michael would inherit something of the values characteristic of northern England at that time, including a dogged persistence, which was needed for survival in the inhospitable world of Mallerstang, Wild Boar Fell, and their environs. That doggedness is still visible in the construction of dry stone walls and the sturdily built houses able to withstand the fierce winds that roar off the mountains, especially that known locally as the Helm. It may also be seen in the persistence Michael Faraday showed in his laboratory, working for long hours each day, for days on end, and in the face of unknown but formidable difficulties.

From his northern family Faraday would have received more than a bullish determination not to give up. There was also the value of hard manual work, manifest daily in the smithy. Faraday did not believe that such hot, sweaty labor was in some way degrading, as many natural philosophers of his day would have felt. He expressed his affection and respect for his father and all that he did at work. It is likely that in that smithy he learned something of a technique in handling materials, as well as how ovens were constructed and operated. No one could have achieved Faraday's impressive scientific accomplishments without a superb experimental technique, and northern elements in his background may well have helped him develop this, and at the very least encouraged him to continue when others would have called it a day.

Perhaps the most persistent element in the northern values—though by no means exclusive to them—is a love of nature. Nature in Mallerstang would have been seen at different times as beautiful, powerful, varied, bountiful, exciting, and menacing; something to be understood rather than tamed, but always *there,* and far more enduring than human lives. But there was another factor that helped to form the values of all the Faradays and to shape the destiny of their most famous son: their religion.

Very near the center of Kirkby Stephen is the parish church in which Richard Faraday had married Mary Hastwell and where, nine years later, James married her sister Margaret. It was then legally necessary that all marriages should take place in the Church of England. However, nearby was a chapel belonging to the local members of a small Christian group known as Sandemanians, after their founder Robert Sandeman (who had died in 1771). This chapel, rather than the parish church, was the spiritual home of both Faraday families.

Throughout the 18th century, England had been experiencing revivals of religion in which many ordinary folk discovered a meaning and a relevance in the Bible that they had not recognized in the formal services of the Church of England. John and Charles Wesley and George Whitefield became world-famous preachers, but there were many others. What all had in common was a respect for the Bible as God's Word, which they recognized as a greater authority than all the traditions of the established churches. The union of church and state as embodied in the Church of England had for two or three centuries posed a particular problem. This kind of arrangement could not be found in the Bible, and those who declined to submit to the Church of England were known as nonconformists or dissenters. Prominent among these in the north of England in the mid-18th century were followers of the erstwhile clergyman Benjamin Ingham, a former colleague of the Wesleys. In Scotland a similar movement was started by the Presbyterian minister John Glas, and the Glasite denomination that he founded was given additional impetus by the weighty theological writings of his son-in-law Robert Sandeman. In 1760 many followers of Ingham joined the resultant Sandemanian church and though Inghamite numbers soon went into steep decline, the Sandemanians prospered, not least in the corner of England inhabited by the Faradays.

The Faraday family had a long tradition of religious dissent. Robert Faraday, Michael's grandfather, had at first inclined to the small group of churches led by Ingham, and had taken his first three children to be christened at the Inghamite Chapel in Kendal, 25 miles from home. When numerous members of that sect had turned (or been led) to the very similar Sandemanian alternative in 1760, Robert joined the Sandemanian Chapel at Wenning Bank, Clapham. In the simple devotions of that church, with its appeal to biblical authority and its high ethical demands, the children of Robert Faraday were reared. They also practiced a literal imitation of Jesus, who once washed his disciples' feet. Each member staunchly maintained his faith, in ethical conduct, in theological belief, in group loyalty, and even in the manner of naming his children.

A sect of German Christians practice foot-washing, a ceremony to imitate the washing of the first disciples' feet by Jesus. In the 17th and 18th centuries several Christian groups including the Sandemanians practiced this ritual.

When Michael Faraday was asked about his religion later in his life, he replied, "I am of a very small and despised sect of Christians known, if known at all, as Sandemanians, and our hope is founded on the faith that is in Christ." He had embraced the faith of his father and uncle that had flourished in Wenning Bank and then Kirkby Stephen, and this faith was to have profound effects in every area of his life. Certainly it was a faith that permeated his family in the years up to and far beyond his birth. And it formed a strong but intangible link with relatives far away when James Faraday made the momentous decision to uproot himself from the familiar scenes of Mallerstang and seek a new life in the unimaginably different environment of London.

The reasons for the Faradays' astonishing migration are not entirely certain. It is fairly clear that James Faraday's health was not good, and overwork at times and a dire shortage of business at others may have damaged it. Outhgill had boasted an ancient inn, the King's Head, and there James Faraday would have heard travelers' tales of the great metropolis and perhaps, like many rustic Englishmen, resolved to seek his fortune in its golden streets. Moreover, since the 1770s Britain had not been able to produce enough grain to feed its citizens, and food was in short supply. With the birth of Elizabeth and Robert, the family may have been in some despair. In 1791, it became clear that a third child was on the way and it was possibly this event that triggered their decision to go. James was doubtless encouraged by Sandemanian contacts in London; by February 20 he had joined the Sandemanian congregation meeting in Paul's Alley, near the Barbican in the old City of London. He set up shop in what was then the suburban village of Newington Butts, near Walworth, in Surrey. In the rooms that James and Margaret had taken next to the smithy, their third child was born on September 22. According to the habit of the Sandemanians, he was given the first name of his mother's father: Michael.

CHAPTER

3

In London: The Bookbinder's Apprentice

Little is known of Michael Faraday's early years. His formal education was sketchy at best. He once wrote: "My education was of the most ordinary description, consisting of little more than the rudiments of reading, writing, and arithmetic at a common day-school. My hours out of school were passed at home and in the streets." We do not even know the name of the school.

With the move to London, it might have seemed that the family's troubles were over. But it was not so, as Britain itself continued to struggle through hard times. The French Revolution had broken out in 1789 and the Napoleonic Wars began in 1793. They heralded an acute trade depression, which made importing food into Britain increasingly difficult. In 1794 and 1795 two poor harvests created shortages on a national scale. Wheat prices increased in one year from 52 to 75 shillings per quarter ton; at times no grain at all could be had, and the cost of other subsistence foods rose as well. Panic set in, fanned by false reports of a deadly

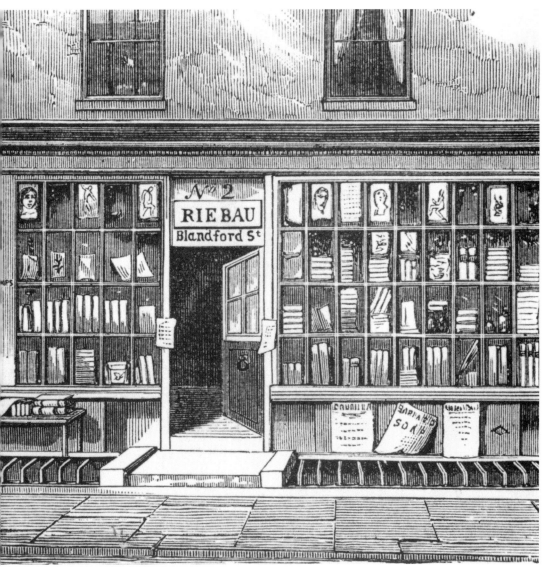

At Riebau's bookshop in London's West End, Michael Faraday labored as a bookbinder's apprentice and discovered much about science from the volumes he encountered.

blight killing the wheat then growing in the fields. Hungry Britons attacked King George III's state coach in London, and the government reacted as though the entire country were under siege. In 1799 and 1800 Britain suffered another pair of disastrous harvests, and wheat prices soared to a staggering 120 shillings. In 1801 the Faradays applied for public relief; Michael had to make one loaf last a week. Within a year the fourth child, Margaret, was born, named after her mother according to Sandemanian custom.

In these difficult years James Faraday's health was declining, and he was capable only of light, part-time work. There was much family hardship. Since 1796 they had lived over a coach-house in Jacob's Well Mews, Charles Street, Manchester Square, as James Boyd, a fellow Sandemanian from Scotland, had given Michael's father work at his smithy and ironworks at Welbeck Street, just around the corner. But business was bad, as fewer horses needed to be shod, and feed prices rocketed upward. So, in 1804, as soon as he was old enough, young Michael Faraday was sent to work for a nearby bookseller and bookbinder, a French émigré named G. Riebau. Riebau hired Michael to deliver newspapers—and collect them after they had been read. Little did anyone guess the consequences of such humble employment.

Michael Faraday quickly impressed his employer, perhaps because of his willingness to work hard, or his sense of fun and good humor despite adversity, or his wonder at the world of books and his growing love for them. But whatever the cause, within a year the boy was accepted as an appren-

Michael spent his first years on Jacob's Well Mews, a back street off London's Manchester Square. The Faraday family lived over the coach-house.

tice to G. Riebau in the ancient craft of binding books. Unfortunately, he no longer received a wage for his work, but he was able to live in a tiny room above the shop. Two weeks later, Lord Horatio Nelson's naval victory over France at the Battle of Trafalgar ended Napoleon's hope of invading Britain. It is arguable that the introduction of Michael Faraday to the world of books, scholarship, and science was equally important to the course of human history.

In 1809 the family moved again, to No. 18 Weymouth Street, near Portland Place. The following year the ailing James Faraday died. He was long remembered with affection by his famous son. Once, many years later, Michael was on holiday at Interlaken in Switzerland and was most interested to observe one aspect of local industry. He wrote: "Clout nailmaking goes on here rather considerably, and is a very neat and pretty operation to observe. I love a smith's shop and everything relating to smithery. *My father was a smith.*"

In 1810 Michael entered his final year as Riebau's apprentice, while his brother had taken a job as a laborer in a new industry that was transforming the face of London: the manufacture and distribution of coal gas. All attended the Sandemanian meetinghouse, where the older sister Elizabeth soon found a husband (the saddler Adam Gray) and where Michael was later to declare his own faith. Margaret, only eight when her father died, became devoted to Michael, who taught her to read and write and whom she sorely missed on his later journeys. By all accounts the bereaved family was still a happy one, presided over by a competent and loving mother. It seems clear that Michael coped with hardship because the Sandemanians tended to view it as a blessing rather than a curse. And, after all, his mother was also one of those "hard progeny of the North."

With his apprenticeship at Riebau's bookbinding establishment, Faraday found himself in a surprisingly congenial situation. His two fellow apprentices were agreeable company, and his master a kindly and skillful teacher. Books that had to be bound included collections of pamphlets, personal notebooks, and old books that were falling to pieces and needed to be bound again. In those days, books were expected to last for generations.

Although little is known about the details of Faraday's apprenticeship, it clearly showed impressive results. Many books that he bound survive today, and they testify to the high quality of his work. Among the processes involved in bookbinding was a prolonged hammering of the pages together, and Faraday once claimed he could apply 1,000 hammer blows without stopping. (Perhaps he was inspired by his father's example at the smithy.) He also exhibited a meticulous neatness in sewing the leaves together and in lettering the finished book on its spine. He would certainly not be the first apprentice to find that learning to use his hands and develop manipulative skills would stand him in good stead in a scientific career in later years.

Yet Faraday was deeply dissatisfied. The acquisition of bookbinding skills, though worthy in itself, was never going to fulfill a need of which he was rapidly becoming aware. Surrounded by books all day at his work, he began to long for knowledge and for an encounter with truth about nature, just as his Sandemanian faith assured him of access to truth about God. It was as though Sandemanianism and science could be twin partners in an enterprise that had been recommended long ago by philosopher Francis Bacon, who wrote of the two "books" of Scripture and nature. Many years later Faraday himself spoke of "the book of nature" that was "written by the finger of God." But how was a poorly educated son of an impoverished blacksmith to attain such knowledge? Where could he begin?

In fact the answer lay all around him—in the books he had to bind and in the books in the shop and in Riebau's library, which he eventually was permitted to use. By great good fortune, in 1809 he lighted on a book that had just been reprinted and which was to serve as an introduction to the whole quest on which he was about to embark. Its title could not have been more appropriate: *The Improvement of the Mind*. It was a famous work by a man well known not as a philosopher or scientist but as a writer of hymns. Isaac Watts, though not a Sandemanian, might have commended himself to Faraday as a fellow dissenter, for he had been a nonconformist minister in the early 18th century. Among this book's recommendations were assiduous reading, attendance at lectures, correspondence with others of similar mind, formation of discussion groups, and the keeping of a "commonplace" book in which to record facts and opinions that might otherwise be forgotten. Within a few weeks the industrious Faraday had begun a commonplace book of his own, formidably entitled *The Philosophical Miscellany*.

Faraday's new quest for knowledge demanded that he read books in abundance. One of the most significant books to come to his notice was actually one that he was binding: a volume of the *Encyclopaedia Britannica*. It contained a very long article on electricity, which immediately aroused the young apprentice's curiosity. Although written by a relatively unknown chemist, James Tytler, the article showed the influence of other writings, notably Joseph Priestley's famous *History and Present State of Electricity* (1767). It hinted broadly to Faraday that the established view of electricity as a single fluid might be wrong and encouraged him to think deeply on that subject for many years. It would be the topic for the first lecture he ever gave to fellow apprentices and others in 1810.

But his earliest scientific passion was not to be in electricity but in chemistry, to which he was led by two very different books. He managed to acquire Thomas Thomson's four-volume *System of Chemistry* (1807), a book intended for expert readers, or at least for those with some training in chemistry. It was notable for offering the first printed account of John Dalton's famous theory of atoms—namely, that all elements are composed of tiny particles of the same weight—not a subject for a novice! Very different was the chatty and popular book *Conversations in Chemistry* (1806) by Jane Marcet, which was specifically intended for the new popular audience for chemistry created partly by the fashionable lectures at the Royal Institution and elsewhere. For Faraday, Mrs. Marcet's book had the great merit of linking chemistry to electricity, thus making it doubly attractive. He was hopelessly hooked.

Another course of action recommended by Watts—to attend classes—was conveniently available to Faraday. Such classes had recently been started by an organization called

Jane Marcet was a successful author of text-books, including Conversations in Chemistry, *which young Michael Faraday first read in 1810 and continued to admire for many years.*

the City Philosophical Society. John Tatum, a progressive and philanthropic silversmith who opened his house in Dorset Street every Wednesday for lectures to young men seeking self-improvement, founded the society in 1808. With a ticket paid for by his brother, Michael Faraday was introduced to the group in February 1810, and here he received his first course in scientific instruction. With almost frightening zeal, he took careful notes from the front row, immediately expanded them into a neater, fuller draft on returning home, and then produced a third version as a full, if not verbatim, account. Tatum was the main lecturer, but at times members of the society were allowed to hold forth on subjects of their choice. That chance came to Faraday in the following spring. His "Lecture on Electricity" was marked by a nervous delivery, meticulous preparation, and a bold attempt to take on the whole scientific community by assailing their views of electricity as a single fluid.

Aware of his defective education, Faraday took other steps toward self-improvement. He engaged the secretary of the City Philosophical Society to coach him in writing skills. The tutor was Edward Magrath, later to become secretary to the exclusive London club the Athenaeum (which Humphry Davy and Michael Faraday would help to found). The lessons continued at two hours a week for nearly seven years. Faraday's literary skills were further developed by a lengthy correspondence with his friend Benjamin Abbott, a clerk in the City. They shared a deep love of science as well as personal piety, and by 1812 the two were meeting frequently, often at Abbott's parents' house.

Life for the young Faraday was not all reading or writing, however. He began to try simple experiments, including work with electricity. The natural substance amber was known to attract lightweight objects like straws when rubbed by certain materials. The phenomenon became known as electricity (from *elektron,* the Greek word for amber) and was studied haphazardly until the 18th century. Many machines were invented to generate this electricity, usually by rubbing a glass or other cylinder that was continuously rotating. By 1745 it was discovered that such electric charges could be stored in a number of devices, such as a bottle of water known as a Leyden jar. This was a primitive condenser. In addition to being produced by friction, electricity could also be obtained from the clouds ("atmospheric electricity"), by heating certain substances (thermoelectricity), and from animals or fish like the electric ray, which administered shocks to other animals ("animal electricity"). But it was not entirely certain that these were all varieties of the same thing.

All these manifestations were later known as "static" electricity, but it had been shown in the 17th century that electricity also could flow (down packthreads or metal wires) and this became known as "current" electricity. In 1791, the year of Michael Faraday's birth, Italian biologist Luigi Galvani discovered accidentally that bodies of dead frogs that were pinned to a metal lattice before dissection would twitch when their muscles were touched with another metal, such as brass. Since the bodies similarly twitched in a thunderstorm, it seemed that electricity was somehow responsible.

This idea led a fellow countryman named Alessandro Volta to conclude that the electricity that caused these convulsions resulted from contact between two dissimilar metals and a moist substance at the same time. He was right. By piling disks made of silver, zinc, and moist cardboard on top of each other, he obtained an electric current when a wire to the zinc disk on the bottom connected the silver one on top. He had invented the first electric battery, and Davy recognized that he had "sounded an alarm-bell to all the experimenters in Europe." Within months two Englishmen, William Nicholson and Anthony Carlisle, had shown that this continuous current could decompose aqueous solutions that it passed through. They had discovered electrolysis.

Intrigued by these efforts, and despite the difficulty of obtaining even the simplest equipment, the young Michael Faraday saved up for a very long time to buy two bottles from an old rag shop. With these he was able to construct a Leyden jar and an electric generator. Later Riebau allowed him to turn one of his workrooms into a laboratory at night, using the fire as a temporary "furnace" and the mantelpiece as a laboratory "bench." Here Faraday constructed a voltaic pile, after Alessandro Volta's. The thrill of discovery as he conducted a few simple experiments with this pile was but a portent of far more exciting things to come. Nor did he limit observations to his "laboratory." In his spare time he would often be seen outdoors, diligently examining industrial processes, in particular the various installations around central London then being developed for treating drinking water.

As the time drew near for Faraday's departure from Riebau, he became increasingly inclined to find employment in science rather than bookbinding. His apprenticeship with Riebau had served him well, but he sought wider horizons. Years later he wrote of "my desire to escape from trade, which I thought vicious and selfish, and to enter the services of Science, which I imagined made its pursuers amiable and liberal." Such idealism cannot have owed much to Sandemanianism, though Sandeman himself was favorably inclined to science. It may reflect Faraday's disenchantment with what he had seen of commercial life in the metropolis. But whatever his motivation, he was determined to leave the world of bookbinding.

He met with several early disappointments. Perhaps the most galling

As a young man, Faraday built this frictional electrical machine, which was typical of many at the time. The action of a leather or other pad rubbing against a rotating glass cylinder generated enough static electricity to yield sparks and electric shocks.

was the fate of a letter written in some desperation to the president of the Royal Society, Sir Joseph Banks. Faraday had asked to be given any situation, however humble, but despite repeated efforts to elicit a response, he was denied the courtesy of even a simple acknowledgment. A circumstance then arose that initially added to Faraday's frustration, but ultimately led to his career in science.

One day during the winter of 1811–12, Riebau happened to show some of Faraday's beautifully inscribed notebooks to a customer, who was deeply impressed. The man showed them to his father, William Dance, a musician who happened also to be a member of the Royal Institution. As a result Faraday received a ticket granting admission to a series of chemistry lectures by the Institution's star performer, the young, ambitious, and vivacious Humphry Davy. Davy's charismatic manner and brilliant delivery were a far cry from the worthy efforts of John Tatum, but Faraday's experience of note-taking at the City Philosophical Society stood him in good stead, and he ended up producing a handsome, 386-page volume, complete with diagrams of apparatuses and experiments. Captivated by Davy's views of the nature of chlorine, Faraday was convinced more than ever that he wanted to be part of this fascinating world of science.

Shortly after these lectures, Davy (who had recently been honored with a knighthood) was injured in an explosion while experimenting on nitrogen trichloride, an accident that nearly cost him his eyesight. While recovering he needed someone to write up his experiments and (possibly on the recommendation of Dance) hired the young Michael Faraday for that purpose. However, he advised Faraday not to leave the bookbinding trade, promising him some business from the Royal Institution. Science, he said, was a harsh mistress. The job as Davy's scribe lasted only a few days, and Faraday did not relish the idea of returning to his prospects as a journeyman bookbinder. He resolved on one final bold action. In late December 1812, he wrote to Davy, seeking his help and enclosing the bound volume of his own notes of Davy's four lectures earlier that year.

Davy, obviously flattered, sent a reply on Christmas Eve:

Sir,

I am far from being displeased with the proof you have given me of your confidence & which displays great zeal, power of memory & attention.

I am obliged to go out of Town & shall not be settled in Town till the end of Jan^y.

I will then see you at any time you wish.

It would gratify me to be of service to you. I wish it may be in my power.

I am Sir

your obedient humble servant

H. Davy

Several weeks later the young man was surprised when a splendid footman came to his door one evening with a message from Sir Humphry Davy requesting Faraday's attendance at the Royal Institution the next morning. Scarcely believing his good fortune, the young bookbinder kept the appointment. Davy informed him that a job had just opened up at the Institution by the dismissal of a brawling laboratory assistant. He then offered Faraday the position, which paid one guinea a week and included board in two rooms, with fuel and light, at the Institution. Not surprisingly, Faraday jumped at the chance and began work in March 1813.

The quarrelsome laboratory assistant inadvertently did immense service not only to Faraday and Davy but to science as a whole.

The American amateur scientist Count Benjamin Rumford founded the Royal Institution in 1799, with the intention of spreading scientific knowledge among all social classes. That philanthropic vision faded rapidly as Humphry Davy's famous discourses attracted the elite of London society.

CHAPTER

4

The Royal Institution

For five or six memorable weeks, Michael Faraday worked for and with Sir Humphry Davy. Among the routine tasks entrusted to him was the preparation of considerable quantities of the compound that had already nearly blinded Davy, nitrogen trichloride. True to form it exploded in Faraday's hands, but because he was wearing a mask the injuries were relatively slight.

Meanwhile, Davy's mind had begun to wander from the work of the Royal Institution. Socialite, keen fisherman, and expatriate Cornishman, he formed a large and convivial party to go fishing in Cornwall, with a little time for exploring the profuse mineral wealth of his native county. Thus began years of touring to satisfy the insatiable ambitions of his new wife, his own thirst for knowledge, and perhaps his vanity as well, for by now his fame had spread and he likely enjoyed the flattering attentions he received wherever he went. After spending 10 years lecturing at the Royal Institution, Davy decided that now it was time for a new beginning. Accordingly, six weeks after engaging Faraday as his assistant, he resigned his professorship at the Institution and became an honorary professor. William

Brande (who had previously taught chemistry at numerous places in London) succeeded him as professor of chemistry.

After Davy left on his Cornish trip, Faraday spent the next few weeks attending lectures and forming his own opinions as how best to use this medium of instruction. And of course he continued his work at the Royal Institution, though Brande rather than Davy now supervised it. Faraday's grasp of chemistry was rapidly expanding.

On Davy's return to London, it was clear that an ambitious—even outrageous—project was in his sights. Although Britain was engaged in a bitter war with France, Davy proposed a tour of Europe that would take him to the heart of the enemy's territory. He wanted to examine the volcanoes of the Auvergne, a mountainous district in the south of France, and northern Italy, mainly to establish his thesis that their activity could somehow be explained in terms of chemical reactions. Impressed by this idea some years before, the Emperor Napoleon had actually granted Davy a passport and permission to pass freely through France, even at the

This cartoon by English caricaturist James Gillray satirically depicts a Royal Institution lecture by Humphry Davy (right, behind desk) on the newly discovered nitrous oxide, or laughing gas. A good time was clearly had by all.

height of its hostilities with Britain. Davy invited Faraday to accompany him and his wife as Davy's assistant, though that task was soon expanded. At the last moment, Davy's valet declined to travel, having fallen a victim to his wife's understandable apprehensions. So his responsibilities also fell on Faraday's unwilling shoulders, but Davy promised that this would be only a temporary arrangement until a full-time valet could be found in Paris.

On October 13, 1813, they set out on their journey to the port of Plymouth from which they would cross the English Channel to France. Faraday, who had never been farther than 12 miles from London and was largely ignorant of his own country's topography, marveled at Devonshire's "mountains," which were in fact only hills. He concluded the whole expedition was to be "a strange venture." On arrival in Brittany, Faraday was outraged by the officiousness of the customs men, who left nothing to chance in their quest for secret compartments in Davy's carriage, their minute examination of the luggage, and their repeated full-body searches. Minor miracles included the re-assembly of the carriage from its parts and the excellent taste of provincial French food despite the visible squalor of the culinary arrangements. On that point Faraday observed that the dishes "require whilst on the table a dismissal of all thoughts respecting the cooking or the kitchen."

Once in Paris things got better, and Faraday was able to spend time sightseeing, which he did with his usual zest for recorded detail. He maintained a journal and sent a constant stream of letters home. The Sandemanian in him could hardly have been expected to delight in the regal magnificence of great churches like Notre Dame. Indeed it repelled him, suggesting to him that he was like a "tasteless heretic." Those were his words, though they may well have been flung at him by Lady Jane Davy, who had little patience and no sympathy for the proletarian youth employed by her husband. Fortunately science was to provide a needed diversion.

On their continental tour of 1813, Faraday and Davy visited a sugar factory in France, where sugar was crystallized from hot solutions.

One of their earliest visits, on November 13, was to a sugar factory. For years the British blockade had cut off supplies of cane sugar from the West Indies, and since 1811 sugar beet had been grown in France as an alternative source. By now 3 million pounds of the crop were being produced each year. Back at the Royal Institution, Faraday's first task had been to extract sugar from beetroot. Now he was able to see the operation performed on an industrial scale.

More delights were to follow. They attended a lecture by the famous chemist Joseph Louis Gay-Lussac, though Faraday found it difficult to follow the presentation because he was not proficient in French. Davy had brought with him a portable laboratory (a common item in those days) containing numerous chemicals and some simple apparatuses like flasks and blow pipes. He used it whenever he had the opportunity; he would use it in a hotel room or in any of the laboratories whose doors were wide open to him. On November 23, Davy received some visitors, including a Frenchman celebrated for his work on electricity, André-Marie Ampère. They had with them a newly discovered substance, dark and crystalline yet readily turning to a violet vapor on heating. Bernard Courtois, the discoverer, was soon convinced of the similarity between this substance and chlorine. Perhaps it contained chlorine? Within a few days Davy's experiments at his rooms in the Hôtel des Princes had convinced him that it did not contain chlorine but was very similar to it in many ways. Davy determined that it must therefore be a new element, and he christened it "iodine," from a Greek word meaning violet-colored.

There followed a visit to Fontainebleau, near Paris; the Auvergne; and then Montpellier, on the Mediterranean coast, where Davy busied himself for a month analyzing

In his journal Faraday sketched a waterspout (like a tornado over the sea) that he observed when he and Davy were in Genoa in 1814.

seaweeds in the hope of detecting iodine. A visit to Nice was followed by a journey across the southern Alps in treacherous conditions to reach Genoa and eventually Florence. In all this traveling Michael Faraday was constantly observing and recording, whether the archaeology of Nîmes, the bleak climatic conditions, the geological formations by the road, or the views from mountain passes. Yet he wrote in a prosaic manner rather than the poetic style favored by Davy, and he was content with factual remarks like "the view from the elevation was very peculiar and if immensity bestows grandeur was very grand."

The two men resumed practicing chemistry in Genoa with experiments on the torpedo, a fish better known today as the electric ray, for its ability to administer an electric shock. They then went on to Florence, where they conducted the expensive experiment of diamond-burning. The Accademia del Cimento owned a large burning glass or lens, and by using it to focus the sun's rays, Davy was able to burn a diamond to nothing but carbon dioxide, thus confirming that it was in fact a form of the element carbon.

As 1814 slipped by, the party witnessed the return from exile of Pope Pius VII to Rome, and during an excursion to Naples, they climbed Mt. Vesuvius, then a gently smoldering volcano. Other Italian cities visited included Pavia, where Davy and Faraday spent time with Alessandro Volta, the greatest living expert in electrical science. They enjoyed a three-month holiday in Geneva, where Faraday met the professor of physics Auguste de la Rive. That was the beginning of a lifelong friendship with much correspondence between them. It is reported that de la Rive met objections to Faraday's presence at a dinner by saying that if Faraday was not allowed to join them, there would be a separate party especially for him. After further relaxation in the Austrian Tyrol, the party returned to Italy for the winter, where Davy continued his chemical analysis of objects from antiquity, particularly pigments like Tyrian purple, which once was used to dye the robes of Roman emperors. It was at Rome that winter that Faraday became thoroughly disenchanted with the tour, and expressed his objections for the first time.

There were many of them. He spoke neither Italian nor French. The Catholicism of Italy was quite incompatible with his own Sandemanian faith, and he longed for the company of fellow believers. Davy, despite his promises, had never found a substitute valet, and even the gentle Faraday smarted from the humiliation of this apparent demotion. But above all the problem lay with Jane Davy, described by Faraday as "haughty and proud to an excessive degree and [delighting] in making her inferiors feel her power." When she attacked her husband's "valet," Davy was unwilling or unable to support his assistant. Often, but not always, Faraday's sense of humor saved him from rancor, such as in the following anecdote recounted by Benjamin Abbott:

Alessandro Volta presented this voltaic pile, or battery, to Faraday. In 1800, Volta had discovered that a column of alternating discs of silver, zinc, and damp card stock yielded a continuous current of electricity.

> When in a boat in the Gulf of Genoa a sudden storm of wind (not unusual there) placed them for a time in some danger, . . . she (Lady D.) was so alarmed that she became almost faint and in consequence ceased from talking. This, [Faraday] told me, was so great a relief to him that he quite enjoyed the quiet, and did not at all regret the cause that had produced it, though the situation was for some time critical.

Although he had intended to go on to Constantinople, this crisis probably made Davy decide to return to England. There were also the matters of a fresh outbreak of the plague in Malta and eastern Mediterranean lands and political uncertainty following Napoleon's escape from Elba. Faraday wrote home with immense relief, and the party arrived in London on April 23, 1815.

The journey left an indelible mark on Faraday. Foreign travel was a completely new experience, and it broadened

During his European tour with Humphry Davy, Faraday wrote to a friend: "The constant presence of Sir H. D. is a mine of inexhaustible knowledge and improvement, and the glorious opportunities I enjoy of improving in the knowledge of chemistry and the sciences continually determine me to finish the voyage with Sir H. D."

his mind. The visiting of sites of scientific and historic importance was an education in itself, and he had had the unique opportunity of meeting personally many of the leading scientific men of Europe. Despite the hassle of being a valet and the snobbery of Lady Davy, Faraday was eternally grateful to Sir Humphry and would never hear a word spoken against him thereafter.

With this "improvement" so painfully gained, he was delighted to be reappointed to the Royal Institution in May 1815 as assistant and superintendent of the apparatus of its laboratory and mineralogical collection. A modest increase in salary (to 30 shillings a week) and accommodations at the top of the Institution building on Albemarle Street (before it became the director's residence) may not have seemed commensurate with the skills implied by his new title, but he was content. Responsible for the care of the laboratory and its contents, he was also required to provide analytical and other scientific services to members of the Institution.

This position cemented Faraday's lifelong association with the Royal Institution—a relationship that made a major contribution to his future success as a scientist. No other place on earth would have afforded him the opportunity to spend nearly 40 years following his natural inclination in the matter of research, with a laboratory, an assistant, a library, and an apartment "over the shop" all provided. Moreover, unlike his successor, he was unencumbered by teaching duties and, apart from set-piece lectures at the Institution, able to pursue his work more or less as he liked.

In addition, the Royal Institution provided Faraday with a personal tutor for several years, who had the additional virtue of being one of the leading chemists of his day. That was, of course, Sir Humphry Davy. Although their relationship was later spoiled by animosity and jealousy on Davy's part, it was he more than any other person who pointed Faraday in the right direction, taught him experimental skills, encouraged him in his natural tidy habits, and gave him a model for popular scientific communication. The Royal Institution and Davy's guiding hand were major factors in the scientific growth of Michael Faraday.

The Royal Institution consisted of three areas. There was a basement, which in Faraday's day housed two main rooms. At the rear stood the famous chemical laboratory, linked to a small lecture theater where the kitchens had once been. In place of the former servants' hall in the front of the basement was a room that eventually became Faraday's magnetic laboratory, linked to a small cellar that was once home to a colony of frogs and hence was known as "the froggery." The underground rooms received little natural light, so gaslight was the primary source of illumination. (The magnetic laboratory came to be known, appropriately enough, as "Faraday's darkroom.") On the first floor were an entrance hall, a conversation room for members, and one or two other rooms. From here the grand staircase led to the second floor with its elegant library and entrance to the famous Lecture Theatre. Finally, there was a top floor where the director lived. If the basement was strictly for private research, and the top floor was the director's private accommodation, the first and second floors were eminently public areas. It was in the Lecture Theatre that the public encountered Davy, Faraday, and a long line of their successors. Contrary to what some have suggested, in each of these three "worlds," Faraday was the same person with the same values, even though he behaved differently in each of them.

From 1816 Faraday lived here, high up in the building and free from unwelcome intrusions. He did not lack friends, many of whom he met at the City Philosophical Society. Judging by his correspondence with Benjamin Abbott he was far too busy to be lonely, scarcely having time to accept invitations to dinner. He was not far from his mother, brother, and sisters whom he regularly saw on Sundays. It seems that, though not yet a member, Michael Faraday continued his childhood habit of attending the Sandemanian chapel in Paul's Alley. Week by week he would listen to the reading and exposition of Scripture and add his own melodious contribution to the singing of hymns. Gradually, perhaps imperceptibly, he adopted their values as his own and identified in a deeper way with their community.

The private world of Faraday's home merged inextricably with the private world of his church. His life took an unexpected, and positive, turn when he fell in love with Sarah Barnard, a silversmith's daughter who was a member of his Sandemanian congregation (and nine years Faraday's junior). Faraday had initially rejected the idea of marriage, because it would distract him from his work, even going so far as to compose an unflattering poem on the subject:

> What is the pest and plague of human life?
> And what the curse that often brings a wife?
> 'tis Love.
> What is the power that ruins man's firmest mind?
> What that deceives its host alas too kind?
> What is it that comes in false deceitful guise
> Making dull fools of those that before were wise?
> 'tis Love.

But Faraday's distrust of matrimony vanished when he realized that he loved Sarah, and he pursued her with an energy usually reserved for his scientific inquiries. He was entirely successful, and on June 12, 1821, they married. Since all British marriages at that time had to be licensed by a minister in an Anglican church, the Faradays were compelled to attend the Church of St. Faith in the City of London, where their marriage was registered, although there was no religious service.

The Faradays' union was supremely happy. A letter to Sarah from Michael in the early days of marriage says it all:

> And now, my dear girl, I must set business aside. I am tired of the dull detail of things, and want to talk of love to you; and surely there can be no circumstances under which I can have more right. . . . Oh, my dear Sarah, poets may strive to describe and artists to delineate the happiness which is felt by two hearts truly and mutually loving each other; but it is beyond their efforts, and beyond the thoughts and conceptions of anyone who has not felt it. I have felt it and do feel it, but neither I nor any other man can describe it; nor is it necessary. We are happy, and our God has blessed us with a thousand causes why we should be so. Adieu for to-night . . .

Within days of his wedding, Faraday had sought membership in the Sandemanian church, which his new wife had joined two years earlier. Their marriage may have prompted his action, though when Sarah asked him why they had not talked about his joining he replied, "That is between me and my God." It was, in one sense, the natural conclusion to a process that had begun in childhood, and it meant a very great deal to Faraday. Having been deemed "to understand and believe the TRUTH, and express a readiness to do whatever Christ has commanded" he received the laying on of hands, a holy kiss, and a hearty welcome into the small fellowship of believers. He was greatly sustained throughout his life by his happy marriage to Sarah, as well as his weekly visits to the Sandemanian church. One friend of his, John Tyndall, attributed Faraday's apparently boundless energy and strength during the week to "his Sunday exercises," adding that "he drinks from a fount on Sunday which refreshes his soul for the week."

The young Michael Faraday at the start of his glittering career, probably just after he had joined the Royal Institution.

CHAPTER

5

Early Chemical Experiments

In the 1810s the Royal Institution had been famous for one science: chemistry. That subject had also been the one that first fired Faraday's imagination at the City Philosophical Society. So although he preferred for himself the old name of "natural philosopher," it was in fact through his chemistry that Faraday first caught the attention of the wider scientific community. Apart from the strong chemical tradition in the Royal Institution, there were several other reasons why Faraday found chemistry so compelling.

Chemistry by 1815 was a subject in a state of considerable flux. In the last 40 years it had undergone not one but two major revolutions. The first, known traditionally as "*the* chemical revolution," had been associated with the work of Antoine Lavoisier in France and had redefined those units of science called the chemical elements. Shortly afterward John Dalton proposed his theory that each of these elements consisted of atoms of the same weight and were all identical to each other, but different from the atoms of any other substance (although Faraday at first shared Davy's skepticism about this theory). Given a new clarity about the basic building blocks of chemistry, much progress could be expected in identifying the constituents of a wide variety of familiar substances, from chalk to sugar. The possibility of finding out the truth about matter afforded by the first chemical revolution would have appealed strongly to the Sandemanian in Faraday, committed to a God-given universe whose laws demonstrated both economy and elegance.

The second chemical revolution was quite different from the first, though it was partly dependent on it. In the short term this revolution would have far more important consequences for society than the ideas of Lavoisier, Dalton, or even Davy. This was a new, if limited, application of chemical laws to the large-scale production of commodities in the Industrial Revolution. The great textile mills springing up all over northern Britain in the early 19th century needed vast quantities of soap (for washing their raw materials and products) and glass (to let in daylight). These two materials were made from soda, which had recently become a large-scale product itself. Salt, limestone, and sulfuric acid were needed to make this soda, and vast soda plants began to spring up all over Britain. The element chlorine was found to be wonderfully effective for bleaching the acres of cloth produced daily by each factory, but that too needed sulfuric acid and salt for its production.

It can be argued that the Industrial Revolution was made possible only by the second chemical revolution, which showed that chemistry could be used for the benefit of mankind. Faraday found this philosophy highly congenial to his Sandemanian faith. He spoke of the "gifts of God" bestowed for human benefit, of nature operating "for our good" and of the application of scientific laws to add to human welfare. True, he lived far away from the great centers of engineering and textiles; he shared the Sandemanian contempt for making money for its own sake; and he regarded benefits to the soul of far greater worth than those

The first chemical revolution was initiated with the work of the French chemist Antoine-Laurent Lavoisier. It redefined those units of science called the chemical *elements*. Lavoisier's ideas also confirmed the role that oxygen, one of those elements, played in the process of combustion, hereby discrediting the "phlogistic theory," which postulated that the action of burning a substance released another hypothetical substance called phlogiston.

Lavoisier viewed many of the new gases that had been discovered recently as compounds of other elements with oxygen—in other words, oxides. If these compounds were derived from nonmetals (such as sulfur, nitrogen, and phosphorus), they tended to be acidic, and indeed Lavoisier's word *oxygène* means "acid producer." His list of these gases was far from complete and left open the possibility that several as yet undecomposed bodies might one day be broken down into their elements, some of which would be new.

One of the most dramatic examples of this took place within the walls of the Royal Institution itself. In 1807, Humphry Davy used a technique known as electrolysis to isolate those highly reactive metal elements sodium and potassium, constituents of the familiar materials salt and potash. Other element discoveries soon followed, both in Davy's laboratory and in Sweden, at the hands of J. J. Berzelius. In the first 15 years of the 19th century, the following had all been isolated and recognized as new elements: palladium, cerium, osmium, rhodium, iridium, potassium, sodium, barium, strontium, calcium, magnesium, boron, and iodine (13 out of the total 50 or so elements then known).

Within a few years of Lavoisier's work (and his death in 1794 at the guillotine in the Reign of Terror during the French Revolution), a further development took place in England, with the theories of the

THE FIRST CHEMICAL REVOLUTION

text continued from page 49

Manchester chemist John Dalton. His was the first chemical atomic theory, which proposed that each chemical element consisted of tiny individual particles called atoms, all of which were the same as each other, but different from the atoms of all other elements. If the relative weights of different atoms were known (the atomic weights, in other words) it would thus be possible to analyze a compound and from the proportions by weight of each element determine the ratios of individual atoms (for instance, two of carbon to four of hydrogen).

In the hands of Berzelius particularly, this proved to be a powerful tool to unlock the mysteries of many compounds derived from living organisms and thus known as "organic." Slowly and painfully, a whole new science of organic chemistry began to emerge, while the much simpler inorganic compounds could also yield their secrets in the same way.

The problem in all this was that no one knew for sure what the relative atomic weights actually were. Thus water contains one part by weight of hydrogen and eight parts by weight of oxygen. If there is one atom of each in water, then the atomic weights are respectively 1 and 8. But if there should be *two* atoms of hydrogen and one of oxygen (giving H_2O) their relative weights will be 1 and 16. Who was to say? Only after much more detailed work was performed did a consensus emerge in about 1860 (which gave oxygen a value of 16) and the relative atomic weights could be defined with confidence.

to the body. But nevertheless he remained committed to applying science for human good, and in 1815 that science was most likely to be chemistry.

Faraday's appointment as assistant and superintendent of the Royal Institution's laboratory apparatus and mineralogical collection represented a major advance in his career. While he no longer had the benefits of Sir Humphry Davy's constant and close supervision, there were other compensations—not least being access to the Institution's considerable library of scientific books and periodicals, some quite rare. Few aspiring scientists of his age would have had use of such a laboratory and equipment as he now helped to supervise. And there were lectures to attend and people to meet, all adding to the stimulus for self-improvement that was already intense enough.

Although he was no longer a professor of chemistry at the Institution, Davy continued to serve as a mentor to Faraday during these early years. After their return from Europe, Faraday was given the task of helping Davy in his research on a safety lamp for coal miners. In those days miners often used candles to enable them to see while they were underground. Unfortunately, methane, a gas that often lurks in coal mines, forms a mixture with air that will explode in contact with a flame. This combustibility caused many tragic and often fatal accidents. To solve this dangerous problem, Davy and Faraday conducted an intense research program for a few weeks at the end of 1815. They showed that covering a flame with wire gauze allowed air to enter but did not permit the flame to be transmitted to the surrounding atmosphere. Further experiments followed in 1816.

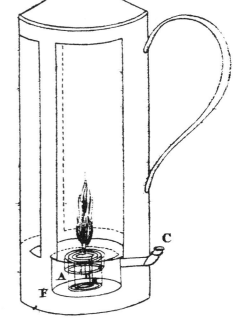

To overcome the danger of inflammable gases in a coal mine being ignited by the flame from a miner's lamp, Humphry Davy devised a safety lamp in which wire gauze windows effectively shielded the flame. Hundreds of lives were saved, though Davy nobly declined to patent his invention.

The whole project was really an early study of flame propagation and gas combustion, far ahead of its time in many respects. It was, for Davy, an unusually systematic program. Faraday helped Davy greatly in this work, and this may well explain the study's methodical character. If true, that would be a major contribution by Faraday to the safety of the miners and the development of the mining industry in Britain, as well as an auspicious start to his research career at the Royal Institution.

Davy's influence also could be readily seen in Faraday's early efforts in chemical analysis. Indeed, his first published paper, in 1816, detailed the results of one of the experiments he had done with Davy during their long European tour. It was an analysis of calcium hydroxide, known to Davy and Faraday as caustic lime, which they found in the hot springs of Tuscany. In Faraday's words, "It was the beginning of my communications to the public, and in its results very important to me." He also acknowledged that Davy had set him to work on the project; indeed Davy added his own conclusions from Faraday's analysis.

In addition, Faraday continued to work with William Brande, Davy's successor as professor of chemistry at the Royal Institution. Brande ran an annual series of lectures on chemistry for medical students, and Faraday assisted him in the preparation of lecture experiments, one of the best ways of learning what actually works in chemistry and what does not. Brande was also the founding editor of the *Journal of Science and the Arts,* in which chemistry featured prominently. Faraday helped him edit this journal, and found himself reading many research papers by chemists far and wide. Nor did he merely glance through them. Editorial work requires minute and critical reading of every sentence, so Faraday's theoretical understanding was helped as much as his practical technique. Meanwhile the young assistant was plowing his way through other journals in the library and taking copious notes in the process. These notes came to be so voluminous that the former bookbinder eventually tore up a copy of William Brande's 1819 textbook *A Manual of Chemistry*, interleaved his own notes within it, and rebound the pages as three volumes.

In July 1819 Faraday turned to a very different kind of task. This was the analysis of iron ores supplied by J.J.

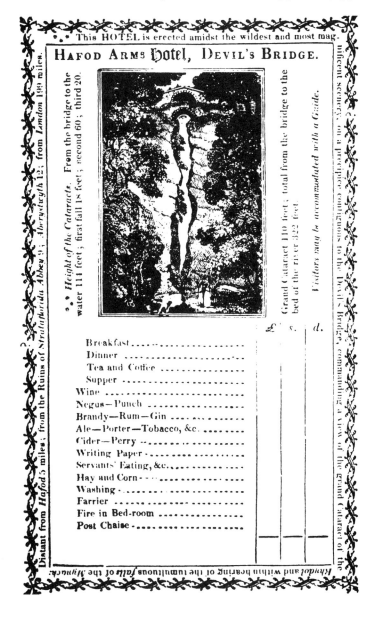

Faraday kept a card from the Hafod Arms Hotel in the western Welsh mountain country as a souvenir of his walking tour of Wales in 1819.

Guest, an ironmaster in Dowlais, South Wales. At Guest's invitation to visit his factory, Faraday and his friend Edward Magrath set off on a walking tour of Wales. In addition to three enjoyable days at Dowlais, they visited Vivian's copper works near Swansea and there learnt of the metallurgy of copper.

Between 1818 and 1822, Faraday assisted James Stodart, one of the Institution's members, with research into alloys of steel. Stodart, a cutlery manufacturer, found an enthusiastic partner in the blacksmith's son. Their goal was to analyze very high-grade steels and reproduce them in the laboratory, but they met with only limited success—until Faraday's visit to the Welsh copper works in 1819. There he had observed that adding a noble metal (such as gold, silver, or platinum) could harden copper. He theorized that the same might hold true for iron as well. He and Stodart alloyed steel with iron by melting the metals in a blast furnace specially designed by Faraday and capable of reaching very high temperatures. But the solution, while possibly sound, proved to be impractical due to the high cost of the noble metals.

By 1819, Faraday had made a reputation as the leading chemist in Britain. He analyzed clays, metal alloys, and other substances, often on a consultant basis. He also was asked to give expert testimony in court cases. The first instance of this occurred in 1820, when he, along with Davy, Brande, Thomas Thomson, and other chemists, was required to testify at the Court of Common Pleas, a civil court in London.

The court was hearing the case of a firm of sugar bakers (concerned with refining raw sugar) whose premises had been destroyed by a fire. Faraday testified on behalf of the insurance companies, who were refusing to pay the claim. The issue was whether the fire had been caused by the ignition of oil used in the process of refining the sugar, or from the ignition of the sugar itself. If the former, the insurance companies argued, then the firm had not reported this hazard and therefore the claim was fraudulent. The sugar bakers declared that the oil would not catch fire at less than 580° F (304° C). Faraday examined large amounts of the oil and showed that it could ignite at considerably lower temperatures. Therefore, he concluded, the oil could indeed have been a material cause of the blaze. The sugar firm was eventually acquitted of fraud, but Faraday's testimony had damaged their case.

This case highlighted three particular points of interest. One was that the defeat of arguments presented by opposing witnesses, and Faraday's growing reputation, probably helped to increase Davy's feelings of jealous rivalry. A rift was already beginning to appear between them. In addition, Faraday's research involved heating the oil and observing its decomposition products, a process that he was soon to apply to other products. Finally, the case exposed the lowly state of the chemist in British society at that time. In order to claim expenses, a witness had to have some professional status (such as law, medicine, or the church). But the court decreed that the chemists' business of "making experiments" was no more professional than that of a mere mechanic, so Davy, Faraday, and the others were denied reimbursement for their expenses. That legal decision stood for many years to come. The subsequent fight for chemists to obtain legal recognition of their professional status took more than half a century to win, though there is a sense in which Faraday and his colleagues had drawn the battle lines in 1820–21.

The year 1821 was a turning point for Faraday as a scientist. His experiments were beginning to shed light on many new aspects of chemistry, including the infant science of organic chemistry, a branch of chemistry concerned with the carbon compounds of living beings and most other carbon compounds. For instance, Faraday wondered why chlorine did not seem to combine with carbon, as most nonmetals did. He conducted a number of experiments between 1821 and 1822 to find out the answer.

Eighteenth-century chemists in the Netherlands had already discovered that ethylene (C_2H_4) would react with chlorine (Cl_2) to produce what was then called "Dutch liquid" ($C_2H_4Cl_2$, now known as a dichloroethane). Faraday showed that exposure of Dutch liquid to an excess of chlorine got rid of all the hydrogen and yielded a substance he called "perchloride of carbon" (C_2Cl_6). Passage of its vapor through a red-hot tube led to another chloride of carbon, C_2Cl_4, which he named "protochloride." Protochloride of carbon, now known as tetrachlorethene, became important as a solvent much used in dry-cleaning. Faraday also produced the iodine counterpart to Dutch liquid by treating ethylene with iodine.

ethylene   Dutch liquid   perchloride   protochloride
                                        of carbon   of carbon

Formation of chlorides of carbon

Another area that he focused on during this period was the study of gases, known as "pneumatic chemistry." What we know today to be separate gases had been thought until the 18th century to be just different kinds of air. But then the chemical individuality of gases was established, and many examples were uncovered by pioneering scientists such as Antoine Lavoisier, Joseph Priestley, Henry Cavendish, and above all the Swedish chemist Carl Wilhelm Scheele, who discovered (and breathed) more new gases than anyone else.

One of Scheele's major findings was that chlorine was a gas. Sir Humphry Davy, who had been the first to recognize chlorine as an element, performed many experiments on the gas and found that it could be combined with water to form a solid he called a "hydrate." One day in 1823, he suggested to Faraday that the solid be heated in a sealed tube. Faraday

did so and observed the formation of an oil. Davy was baf-
fled by this occurrence, as was his dinner-guest that evening,
John Paris, an eminent doctor who would one day write
Davy's biography. How could chlorine, a gas, give rise to an
oil? The only other substance apparently present was water.
The next morning, Paris received the following note:

> Dear Sir,
> The oil that you noticed yesterday turns out to be liquid
> chlorine.
> Yours faithfully,
> M. Faraday

Without realizing it, they had liquefied the chlorine gas
through applying pressure, in this case by heating it in a
closed tube (since the pressure of a gas is proportional to its
temperature). A few cases had been reported in previous
years of gases being liquefied by pressure, but neither Davy
nor Faraday was aware of this when they heated chlorine
hydrate. Within weeks Faraday had liquefied a whole range
of gases by applying pressure to them. He recognized that
for some gases liquefaction was impossible above a certain
temperature, which we call the "critical temperature."
Many years later he combined this pressurizing technique
with that of cooling by the recently discovered solid carbon
dioxide ("dry ice") and thereby discovered several other
gases that could be liquefied at fairly low temperatures.

6

The Beginnings of Electromagnetic Research

Even as Faraday was conducting his experiments in chemistry, he also was researching the principles of magnetic rotation, a line of inquiry that led ultimately to the invention of the electric motor. His interest in the topic was sparked by a change in the way some of his scientific contemporaries were beginning to view the universe.

For centuries, students of nature have argued for a universe in which a few simple laws would explain all events. In the late 17th century, Sir Isaac Newton had shown that one kind of force (namely, gravity) could account not only for an object falling from a table to the floor, but also the movements of planets and stars in the heavens. Around 1800, a new movement, known as Romanticism, gained momentum. Romanticism stressed feelings and values, human beings' unity within nature, and the unity existing within nature. In Germany a version of Romanticism called *Naturphilosophie* evolved, and for all its vagueness and loose thinking, it made the point that forces hitherto regarded as separate might in

For more than 40 years Faraday worked in this study and lived "over the shop," in an apartment on the top floor of the Royal Institution, where he entertained, studied, and found a haven from the distractions of science and the world.

fact be related to one another, or could even be different manifestations of the same underlying power.

Natural magnets have been known since antiquity. But the scientific study of magnetism really began with the English physician William Gilbert, who wrote *De Magnete, Magneticisque Corporibus, et de Magno Magnete Tellure* (On the Magnet, Magnetic Bodies, and the Great Magnet the Earth), the first treatise on magnetism, in 1600. Among many other things, he studied lodestones (natural magnetic minerals) and concluded that the earth itself was a magnet. The way the earth's magnetism varied over its surface was examined by many other men of science, which resulted in the beginning of the science of geomagnetism. By the 18th century, a series of quantitative experiments culminated in the work of French physicist Charles-Augustin de Coulomb, who showed that the force between magnetic poles was inversely proportional to the square root of the distance between them.

One of the early proponents of Romanticism was the Dane Hans Christian Ørsted, who from 1806 had been professor of physics at the University of Copenhagen. He had attempted to prove the unity of magnetic and electric forces in a lecture demonstration in April 1820. By placing a magnetic compass (still in its glass case) immediately below a thin platinum wire, and passing an electric current through the wire, he observed a small but definite deflection of the compass needle. He published the result of this experiment three months later, including remarks about the direction of deflection, the unimportance of the material of the wire or the presence of intervening objects, and a rather puzzled speculation that the cause might be some kind of circular force surrounding the wire.

His paper created a stir across Europe. Similar experiments were attempted by many notable men of science, including André-Marie Ampère, who showed that if a current passes through two parallel electric wires near each other, they do not stay parallel for very long. If the cur-

DIFFERENT KINDS OF MAGNETS

All magnets will always point north-south if freely suspended in the absence of other magnets. This is because they tend to align themselves with the earth's magnetic field. Each magnet has two poles, north and south, and each pole attracts the opposite pole in another magnet and is repelled by a similar one.

The earth: The earth is an immense natural magnet, whose north pole attracts the south pole of a compass needle or other magnet. The geographical and magnetic poles do not quite coincide, but allowance can easily be made for the slight differences of direction.

Electromagnets: Soft iron cores surrounded by coils of insulated wire through which may flow a direct current. When that happens the iron cores become powerfully magnetized. Their magnetism can thus be switched on or off at will.

Lodestones: Natural magnetic minerals, mainly made of the iron oxide magnetite (Fe_3O_4) found once at Magnesia in Greece—hence the name. These were used for centuries to guide navigators in bad weather when the stars were not visible.

Permanent magnets: Pieces of steel (often containing cobalt) that have been made magnetic by rubbing against other magnets or by the action of electricity. They also point north-south when suspended and do not lose their magnetism unless strongly heated, violently struck, or brought near an even stronger magnet.

Permanent magnets are usually bars, either straight or bent into a horseshoe shape.

Temporary magnets: Usually pieces of soft iron which may be magnetized by rubbing with another magnet or by an electric current. They lose their magnetism rapidly, often as soon as the current is switched off.

rents are both flowing in the same direction, the wires attract each other and move closer together; if the currents are flowing in opposite directions, however, the wires repulse each other and move farther apart.

Meanwhile in London, William Wollaston, a scientific friend of Davy's, had become greatly interested in the new concept of electromagnetism. He suggested that electric current traversed a wire in a spiral manner like a corkscrew, in which case he predicted that such a wire, if freely suspended, should actually rotate in the presence of a magnet. But, he repeatedly failed to achieve this effect.

Faraday, however, was coming to the view that the effect of the magnet would not rotate the wire, but rather move it from side to side. This followed from his conclusion that there were four positions in which each pole of a magnetized needle could respond to the current in the wire, two by attraction (A) and two by repulsion (R). He made a note of this phenomenon in his diary on September 3, 1821:

3. On examining these more minutely found that each pole had 4 positions, 2 of attraction and 2 of repulsion, thus

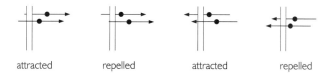

attracted   repelled   attracted   repelled

4. Or looking from above down on to sections of the wire

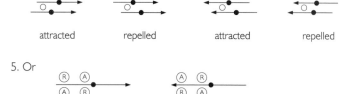

attracted   repelled   attracted   repelled

5. Or

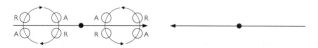

6. These indicate motions in circles round each pole, thus

On September 3, 1821, he managed to prove this theory with an ingenious experiment. Faraday devised a simple apparatus in which a vertical wire, hooked over at the top and with each end dipping into a small amount of mercury, could be connected to an electric battery. When a magnet was brought up to the wire it tried to move either toward or away from the magnet, depending on which pole was presented to it. It did not rotate about its axis as Wollaston had predicted. By bending the wire into a form resembling a crankshaft, and bringing the magnet near the middle, Faraday discovered that the "crank" whirled round so as to get as close to the magnet as possible. If Faraday then reversed the magnet, presenting the other pole to the wire, the crank moved away quickly. By performing this alternation constantly, he obtained continuous motion from the bent wire.

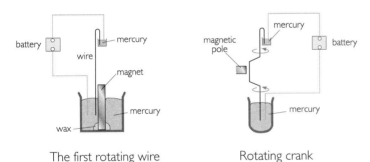

The first rotating wire   Rotating crank

On the following day Faraday showed that a magnet could be made to rotate around an electrified wire, and the day after that he established that a floating magnet could enter a coil of wire through which a current was passing. Within a week or two, Faraday was faced with the problem of inventing a device in which the rotation of both wires and magnets could be demonstrated.

Faraday was not aware of all the activity in Europe on the subject of electromagnetism until, one morning in early October 1821, Sir Humphry Davy, another convert to Romanticism, bounded into the laboratory at the Royal

Institution, bearing news of Ørsted's work and bursting with enthusiasm to repeat the experiments himself. His zest was entirely understandable. If a union of electricity and chemistry was possible, why not one between electricity and magnetism? Davy was far from being the first to suggest such a connection, but its clear demonstration would further reinforce his passionate view of the unity of nature. With Faraday's assistance, he set to work at once.

Repeating Ørsted's experiments was easy; explaining them was not. However, at this particular time Faraday had other things on his mind, not least his research on chlorine. Nevertheless, a request from fellow chemist Richard Phillips for Faraday to contribute an article called "A Historical Sketch of Electromagnetism" to the *Annals of Philosophy* prompted him to embark upon a long series of experiments in which he tried to repeat all the major work of Ampère and others and at the same clarify his own views. Far from convinced by explanations that assumed that electricity was a material substance, or that it existed in two forms, positive and negative, Faraday could only get as far as the view that

A copper conductor is inserted through the bases of two glass cups containing mercury. In the one on the left, a cylindrical magnet is anchored to the copper by a thread and protrudes through the mercury surface. The left-hand arm of the central brass pillar extends to reach the mercury. In the right-hand cup, the magnet is held rigidly vertical and a stiff but movable wire is attached to the brass stand above. An electric current may pass by connecting the brass pillar and the copper conductor to the poles of the battery (not seen here), causing the magnet to rotate around the brass in the first cup, and the electrified wire to rotate around the magnet in the second.

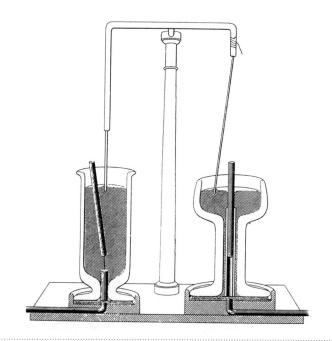

passage of electricity created a *state* in the wire that would somehow affect a magnetic needle. That this effect was much more complex than he or anyone else had imagined began to emerge from the few curious results he had obtained in September.

Other commitments claimed his attention for the next few weeks, but by late December he had returned to electromagnetism, improving the suspensions of rotating wires and showing that even the earth's weak magnetism was enough to swing horizontal wires when electrified. Faraday also made another, more portable, version of the rotating-wire equipment and sent it to other scientists. This not only symbolized his deep conviction as to the importance of scientific communication, but was also a tangible demonstration of his greatness as a scientific discoverer. On Christmas Day, Faraday was hard at work again. He showed that terrestrial magnetism was able to produce a continuous rotation of a wire suspended at an angle greater than the angle of dip of a compass needle. His wife's brother, George Barnard, witnessed the experiment:

> All at once he exclaimed, 'Do you see, do you see, do you see, George?' as the wire began to revolve. One end I recollect was in the cup of quicksilver, the other attached above to the center. I shall never forget the enthusiasm expressed in his face and the sparkling in his eyes!

Even Sarah Faraday was summoned to witness the triumph, despite her protestations that their first Christmas goose would be burned. Faraday's successes in the fields of gas liquefaction and magnetism pleased him greatly, but they also led to some acrimony. When Faraday published his report of revolving wires in October 1821, Wollaston became incensed. It was widely known that he, Wollaston, had predicted that an electrified wire would move when exposed to a magnet; he simply had not proved it yet. In his mind, Faraday had stolen his thunder, if not his actual idea, and he let others, including his friend Davy, know of his anger.

The accusation of plagiarism devastated Faraday, an understandable reaction given his strong Sandemanian faith. He had tried to communicate with Wollaston before publishing his paper, on the grounds that he might find the results interesting. Wollaston was not in town, however, and Faraday, believing that one secret of success was "Work, finish, publish," went ahead. For the rest of his days he regretted his decision not to delay publication until he met with Wollaston. He sought to speak to the aggrieved experimenter after the paper came out, but received only a cold rebuff.

In fact Faraday was technically in the right. Wollaston had predicted that the wire would rotate about its axis, which was not the case. Faraday, on the other hand, was concerned with the wire's revolution about a magnetic pole, a subtle but definite difference. The quarrel might have ended there had not Davy also accused Faraday of plagiarism in 1823. Faraday had published a paper on the results of his gas liquefaction experiments listing himself as the sole author. Davy was seriously annoyed because he felt he should be given co-credit.

The outraged Davy went so far as to attempt to block Faraday's candidacy for the Royal Society, the leading scientific organization in Britain. Davy's opinion would have carried a great deal of weight, as he was president of the society at the time. Richard Phillips and 28 others recently had nominated Faraday, and his nomination certificate was displayed in the society as custom dictated. Not long after the certificate went up, a rather nasty scene took place between the two men, as described by Faraday:

> Sir H. Davy told me I must take down my certificate. I replied that I had not put it up; that I could not take it down, as it was put up by my proposers. He then said I must get my proposers to take it down. I answered that I knew they would not do so. Then he said, I as President will take it down. I replied that I was sure Sir H. Davy would do what he thought was for the good of the Royal Society.

Davy agitated against Faraday's membership, stating publicly on many occasions that his assistant had transgressed the rules of plagiarism with respect to both his and Wollaston's work. It is hard to conceive any reason for this other than pique and possibly envy. However, in this case the members went against the wishes of their president, electing Faraday almost unanimously.

Davy's vengeful petulance was matched only by Faraday's magnanimity, for no word against his former patron was ever permitted in his presence. Only once was he goaded into defending himself, and that was following the publication in 1836 of a biography of Humphry Davy by his brother, John. Speaking of the controversy, John Davy remarked, "I am surprised that Mr. Faraday had not come forward to do him [Davy] justice," an acknowledgment being "necessary to his own honest fame." Faraday responded, in a letter to the *Philosophical Magazine,* that Davy never told him *why* he suggested the experiment on chlorine hydrate, and that Faraday had acknowledged Davy's suggestion in his paper. He also pointed out that the paper had been published in the journal *Philosophical Transactions of the Royal Society,* so Davy, as the society's president, could certainly have vetoed its publication. Indeed, Davy even appended a note of his own.

If Faraday was guilty of anything in this sad story, it would be of violating a scientific etiquette that is now long dead, and was nebulous even at the time. This seemed to have demanded a far greater consultation with only marginally interested parties (Wollaston and Davy) before publication than is now the case. Faraday wisely put these controversies behind him and continued to distinguish himself in his scientific career.

Faraday lectures to an audience including children, several distinguished scientists, and the Prince Consort and the Prince of Wales at the Royal Institution in December 1855. The British Quarterly Review reported: "He had the art of making philosophy charming, and this was due in no little measure to the fact that to grey-headed wisdom he united wonderful juvenility of spirit."

Chemistry and Communication

In 1823 Brande was unable to deliver one of his lectures and Faraday was asked to fill in unexpectedly. In the small lecture room attached to the laboratory, he thus began a career of scientific communication at the Royal Institution that lasted for almost 40 years. He had had some practice at the City Philosophical Society, having delivered a course of 17 lectures on chemistry by the end of 1818. In addition, he had been coached in public speaking by his friend Edward Magrath, and even attended an evening class in elocution. Faraday would have been forgiven for attaching little importance to this event in 1823. After all, what was one lecture in a small room, given to probably unreceptive medical students?

Perhaps as a response to that solitary lecture in 1823, it was announced in 1824 that two extended and practical courses of lectures in chemistry would be delivered by William Brande *and* Michael Faraday. A similar cooperative venture was announced for each of the next three years. The end of the arrangement might have been connected with a row between Brande and the Institution's managers over his editing of their journal. They thought he treated it

The arrival of gas lighting on Pall Mall, one of the first streets in the world to be illumined by gas-light (1807), created a stir in London among all social classes. Gas obtained by heating coal could now be piped from the gasworks to locations some distance away.

almost as his private property. Despite the fact that Brande was working nearby as resident consultant at the Royal Mint in 1825, he remained a largely absentee professor at the Royal Institution until 1852.

Around this time, Faraday discovered a new focus for his chemical research: liquids associated with the new illuminating gas industry. These fluids—materials of great importance to society but of largely unknown character—urgently required analysis. Not the least important of these was whale oil, which was used in gas lighting.

To produce the gas for lighting, whale oil was heated until it decomposed into many gaseous products. When compressed to a pressure of 20 or 30 atmospheres, the gases occupied far less volume and could be easily transported in sealed copper cylinders. About 20 percent of the gases condensed to a liquid, and Faraday began to experiment with this liquid in 1825. He gradually heated the oil so that as the temperature rose, a succession of different products boiled off and were condensed at 32° F (0° C). White crystals formed as a result, and Faraday isolated and examined them. These crystals turned out to be what we know today as benzene.

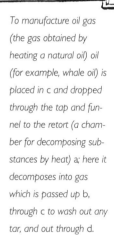

To manufacture oil gas (the gas obtained by heating a natural oil) oil (for example, whale oil) is placed in c and dropped through the tap and funnel to the retort (a chamber for decomposing substances by heat) a; here it decomposes into gas which is passed up b, through c to wash out any tar, and out through d.

This discovery was a remarkable achievement. The isolation of benzene by Faraday's technique is not easy even using modern equipment, let alone with the simple apparatus at Faraday's disposal: just a few small flasks, a thermometer, and a condenser. Repetition of this work nearly 150 years later, with sophisticated instruments, confirmed that many of the products Faraday had reported (which included isobutylene as well as benzene) were in fact present—a powerful tribute to Faraday's superb experimental technique.

It is hard to exaggerate the importance of Faraday's discovery of benzene. Literally tens of thousands of useful substances were derived from it. Such "aromatic" chemicals, as they were called, are still often made from benzene today.

In addition to whale oil, coal gas was another form of fuel used for lighting in the 19th century. It made a bright flame when burned and could be carried great distances through iron pipes, leading rapidly to the establishment of street-lighting in the major towns and cities of Britain. In the making of coal gas large quantities of other substances accumulated, not least vast amounts of black, oily coal tar. New organic products (such as naphthalene) could be obtained from coal tar, and Faraday analyzed these.

In 1825 Faraday became director of the laboratory,

although he still assisted Brande in his lectures to medical students. Upon his appointment he determined to share his knowledge and love of science with a wider audience. At once he invited members of the Royal Institution to attend meetings in the laboratory, where Brande lectured during the day. Three or four meetings took place in 1825, one of which was on "electromagnetic rotations."

That same year he received an important commission. The Royal Society, acting on behalf of the British government, invited Faraday to undertake research into the optical properties of the glass used in telescopes. The problem was that glass used in precision optical instruments had to be homogeneous, with no local concentration of any one ingredient and no bubbles or striations. Faraday's assignment was to figure out how to produce glass to those specifications.

Faraday, along with the astronomer John Herschel and the optician George Dolland, spent much time examining

During the late 1820s Faraday had improved on the glass used for lenses; 15 years later in his experiments on diamagnetism he used specimens of heavy glass such as this.

the process of manufacturing glass. In 1827, Faraday was provided with a special furnace at the Royal Institution, together with an assistant, Sergeant Charles Anderson, whose job was to perform the routine tasks of preparing ingredients and determining specific gravities. Faraday's first experiments were not encouraging. Any attempts to stir the molten glass (to get rid of bubbles and other imperfections) shattered the earthenware pots in which it was being heated. Using pots made of platinum foil produced better results, although as often as not the expensive platinum was destroyed by hot lead oxide that had escaped onto the heated plate.

Faraday made some progress by adjusting the temperature and varying the ingredients, particularly replacing the lead component of the glass, its oxide, by a more complex lead compound, its borosilicate. Further disappointments lay ahead, however, including the formation of colored glass. Eventually the cause was identified as the presence of lead, resulting from reduction of a lead compound by carbon monoxide (from carbon in the cast-iron pan). Replacement of the iron by heat-resistant stone solved the problem, and by 1829 Faraday had ironed out all of the other difficulties as well. As a result, he was able to report success later that year at a Bakerian Lecture to the Royal Society that required three evenings to deliver.

Faraday's optical glass research is a classic example of a scientist performing painstaking empirical investigation, methodically eliminating one possibility after another, though without using any elaborate theory as a guide. While it did not lead to any immediate or dramatic improvement in the quality of glass used for lenses, the introduction of borosilicates was to prove useful both for later glass manufacturing and in some of Faraday's own experiments many years in the future. The most immediate result was that the Royal Institution gained much-needed funds and Faraday a wider reputation for his careful research.

In 1826 Faraday inaugurated the regular Friday evening discourses (lectures) that continue at the Royal Institution to this day. During the first year, Faraday himself delivered three discourses, on caoutchouc (native rubber), on Sir Marc Isambard Brunel's gas engine, and on the theory of lithography. For 36 years he would give some 100 discourses, attracting an audience of rarely less than 500, and 1,000 or more on three occasions when the topic was magnetism.

The year 1827 was an important one for Faraday's lecturing career. Apart from the Friday discourses on magnetism, chlorine as a disinfectant, and the Thames Tunnel, he also offered a short course entitled "Some General Points of Chemical Philosophy." As if he was not busy enough with his normal duties, he added a course of 12 lectures at the London Institution (the poor man's equivalent of the Royal Institution) on "Chemical Manipulation," which later appeared as a very influential book. And at the very end of the year he launched the Royal Institution's "Christmas Lectures," which quickly became an annual event. The opening series was "A course of six elementary lectures on Chemistry, adapted to a juvenile audience," commencing at 3 P.M., an hour appropriate for children. Through such actions, Faraday laid the foundation for popular scientific communication that continues in Britain to the present day.

All reports of Faraday's lectures convey the impression of an outstanding lecturer who knew exactly what he was doing and did it superbly. He paid attention to his speaking technique. He left among his manuscripts the following rules:

> Never repeat a phrase.
> Never go back to amend.
> If at a loss for a word, not to ch–ch–ch or eh–eh–eh,
> but to stop and wait for it. It soon comes, and the bad
> habits are broken and fluency soon acquired.
> Never doubt a correction given to me by another.

By avoiding conventional mannerisms of rhetoric or convoluted logic, he was in fact reproducing the style of the

Royal Institution of Great Britain,

ALBEMARLE STREET,

December 3, 1827.

A

COURSE OF SIX ELEMENTARY LECTURES

ON

CHEMISTRY,

ADAPTED TO A JUVENILE AUDIENCE, WILL BE DELIVERED
DURING THE CHRISTMAS RECESS,

BY MICHAEL FARADAY, F.R.S.

Corr. Mem. Royal Acad. Sciences, Paris ; Director of the Laboratory, &c. &c.

The Lectures will commence at Three o'Clock.

Lecture I. Saturday, December 29. Substances generally—Solids, Fluids, Gases—Chemical affinity.

Lecture II. Tuesday, January 1, 1828. Atmospheric Air and its Gases.

Lecture III. Thursday, January 3. Water and its Elements.

Lecture IV. Saturday, January 5. Nitric Acid or Aquafortis—Ammonia or Volatile Alkali—Muriatic Acid or Spirit of Salt—Chlorine, &c.

Lecture V. Tuesday, January 8. Sulphur, Phosphorus, Carbon, and their Acids.

Lecture VI. Thursday, January 10. Metals and their Oxides—Earths, Fixed Alkalies and Salts, &c.

Non-Subscribers to the Institution are admitted to the above Course on payment of One Guinea each ; Children 10s. 6d.

[Turn over.

This handbill advertised Faraday's first set of Christmas Lectures. The lectures continue to this day as an annual television series, and are a very early example of popular science education for young people.

best preachers in his Sandemanian church (who showed none of the flourishes of even the greatest preachers like Wesley). He also wrote full notes, as was his custom, and prepared in great detail.

He made a special point of engaging with his audience. This elementary point showed itself in many ways. He began with the familiar; he deliberately avoided technical terms where simpler ones would do; he presumed that his listeners had no previous knowledge of his topic (and he

THE CHEMICAL HISTORY OF A CANDLE

Faraday's most famous Christmas Lecture, "The Chemical History of a Candle," is a magnificent example of imaginative scientific exposition. It started from the familiar, a candle, and led to such concepts as capillary attraction, the causes of luminosity, the nature of combustion, and even the modes of manufacturing candles. The following excerpt is from the opening of that lecture series, which Faraday gave in December 1848. The lecture was published in 1861 and has been reprinted many times over the years. It remains a major influence on chemists right up to the present day.

purpose, in return for the honour you do us by coming to see what are our proceedings here, to bring before you, in the course of these lectures, the Chemical History of a Candle. I have taken this subject on a former occasion; and were it left to my own will, I should prefer to repeat it almost every year—so abundant is the interest that attaches itself to the subject, so wonderful are the varieties of outlet which it offers into the various departments of philosophy. There is not a law under which any part of this universe is governed which does not come into play, and is touched upon in these phenomena. There is no better, there is no more open door by which you can enter into the study of natural philosophy, than by considering the physical phenomena of a candle. I trust, therefore, I shall not disappoint you in choosing this for my subject rather than any newer topic, which could not be better, were it even so good.

And before proceeding, let me say this also—that though our subject be so great, and our intention that of treating it honestly, seriously, and philosophically, yet I mean to pass away from all those who are seniors amongst us. I claim the privilege of speaking to juveniles as a juvenile myself. I have done so on former occasions—and, if you please, I shall do so again. And though I stand here with knowledge of having the words I utter given to the world, yet this shall not deter me from speaking in the same familiar way to those whom I esteem nearest to me on this occasion.

And now, my boys and girls, I must first tell you of what candles are made. Some are great curiosities. I have here some bits of timber, branches of trees particularly famous for their burning. And here you see a piece of that very curious substance taken out of some of the bogs in Ireland, called *candle-wood*, a hard, strong, excellent wood, evidently fitted for good work as a resister of force, and yet withal burning so well that where it is found they make splinters of it, and torches, since it burns like a candle, and gives a very good light indeed. And in this wood we have one of the most beautiful illustrations of the general nature of a candle that I can possibly give. The fuel provided, the means of bringing that fuel to the place of chemical action, the regular and gradual supply of air to that place of action—heat and light—all produced by a little piece of wood of this kind, forming, in fact, a natural candle.

was frequently right in this assumption); he used humor in an especially engaging way; and he never talked down to people. He had Sergeant Anderson raise a card labeled *Slow* or *Time* as appropriate. All these features of his delivery helped him establish a strong rapport with his audience, even with those whose scientific knowledge was so small that all they could reasonably expect was mild entertainment.

He relied on a relentless logic to communicate points to his audience, letting his listeners draw their own conclusions. He did not permit himself to be merely didactic, telling his hearers what he thought they should believe. Such a patronizing approach might win short-term gains, but would be unworthy of both speaker and audience. This characteristic is again reminiscent of the approach Robert Sandeman urged on his followers. In church the conclusions were to be drawn from the Bible; in the scientific discourse they had to be based on experimental facts. A classic example of this rationality was Faraday's devastating critique of the supposed phenomenon of "table turning," the alleged spontaneous movement of tables during the séances practiced in Spiritualist circles. This occurred in a lecture on mental education and also in a letter to the *Athenaeum* in 1853. Though accused by some of materialism—a belief that everything can be ultimately explained in terms of matter alone—he was in fact maintaining the same attitude to superstition as the Sandemanians did to unbiblical church tradition:

> What a weak, credulous, incredulous, unbelieving, superstitious, bold, frightened, what a ridiculous world ours is, as far as concerns the mind of man. How full of inconsistencies, contradictions, and absurdities it is.

He was totally committed to the use of demonstrations. This was not a strong tradition in British science up to that time, but after Faraday the lecture-demonstration was a key to successful teaching of the physical sciences. If he spoke of stones falling, kettles boiling, or candles burning, he always offered actual demonstrations to illustrate his words. He once said, "Take nothing for granted as known; inform the eye at the same time as you address the ear." Often his demonstrations were much more complex than dropping stones or boiling kettles. At one lecture he astounded his audience by taking the Royal Institution's great magnet and hurling at it a poker, a pair of tongs, and an iron scuttle full of coals (all of which adhered completely). At another he placed himself in a wire cage and allowed his assistant to apply an enormous electrical voltage to it. When he emerged unscathed from this "Faraday cage," the spectators were impressed not only by his physical courage, but also by the remarkable properties of electrostatic shields.

In Faraday's lectures at the Royal Institution he often discussed applications of science that could bring material benefit to mankind. If he did not address these commercial, political, and economic issues, it was not because they were forbidden areas for a Sandemanian, but because they were simply irrelevant to his scientific topic. In addition, they might have introduced a needless note of controversy that would have neutralized his efforts to achieve rapport with his audience. But that does not mean that Faraday had no interest in industry, nor that he spent all his working life in an ivory tower (or rather basement) in Albemarle Street. Faraday was frequently consulted on all manner of questions relating to chemistry (and later physics) in the wider world. Throughout his life he served the courts as an expert witness and advised cultural institutions on the preservation of books and works of art. For instance, the Athenaeum Club asked him to advise on two problems caused by its gas lighting: it was making the members drowsy and causing the bookbindings to deteriorate. The latter effect resulted from sulfur dioxide in the atmosphere, and Faraday recommended, among other provisions, much better ventilation for the club's rooms.

Perhaps the most famous of all the gentlemen's clubs in London, the Athenaeum included Davy and Faraday among its founders.

In 1829 Faraday accepted a professorship in chemistry at the Royal Military Academy at Woolwich, where he was required to deliver 25 lectures a year and often spend one or two days a week in term-time. The extra money he earned in this position allowed him to hire Anderson as his permanent assistant. In praise of this faithful retainer, Benjamin Abbott wrote:

> Sergeant Anderson . . . was chosen simply because of the habits of strict obedience his military training had given him. His duty was to keep the furnaces always at the same heat, and the water in the ashpit always at the same level. In the evening he was released, but one night Faraday forgot to tell Anderson he could go home, and early next morning he found his faithful servant still stoking the glowing furnace, as he had been doing all night long.

Anderson proved to be an immense help to Faraday in his experiments, and Faraday always appreciated his contributions. In fact, Anderson was the only person permitted to assist Faraday in new experiments. No research students or

associates were ever employed, as group research was simply not Faraday's style. This was partly because few people could match Faraday's superb experimental technique, nor was it likely that newcomers could adapt to his unsocial hours in the laboratory (he was sometimes known to work from 9 A.M. to 11 P.M.). It may also have been a reaction to his relationship with Davy, which provoked many painful memories. But above all, it probably reflected Faraday's complete lack of worldly ambition: He did not wish—or need—to be known as the founder of any particular research school.

Faraday's indefatigable assistant Sergeant Charles Anderson works in his basement laboratory with its arrays of bottles. Skylights extending beyond the main walls of the building provided the room's only natural illumination.

58 The needle did not remain deflected but returned to its
place each time. The order of motions were given as in
former expts — the motions were in the direction consistent
with former expts i.e. the indicating needle tended to become parallel with the exciting magnet being on the same side of the wire
& poles of the same name in the same direction

59 When the Phelices were made one long helix the effect
was not so strong on the galvanometer as before — probably not
half so strong — So that it is best in pieces & combined at the end

60 When only one of the Phelices was used it was least
powerfull. hardly sensible

61 Made a sort of jacket of tin foil round a paper cylinder
so that being separated at the edges by paper the galvanometer
wires could be attached &c. Then pushed mag-
net in & out but could perceive nothing
at galvanometer. Could hardly indeed expect it because as magnet
introduced there was the part in advance ready to carry the
current back. Now in coil, the part in advance could not &c

&c But jacket may be effectual with iron in its place
made a magnet at once either by contact of bars or by helix
round it

Oct 18. 1831

62 Again charged battery of 12 troughs 10 pr each 4 inches
square

63 Re-experimented with both of coils M. (   ) connected
as before with the galvanometer. When battery was connected with
one wire the other very feebly affected galvanometer. When contact

On October 17, 1831, Faraday recorded wrapping a coil of wire around a paper cylinder and connecting the ends. A needle deflected sharply when he inserted a magnet into the cylinder, suggesting a wave of electricity.

Deeper into Electricity—and Magnetism

In the late 1820s and early 1830s, Faraday began to experience a greater feeling of liberation and adventurousness in his scientific pursuits. This may be partly because of the departure of two figures that had cast a shadow over his life: William Wollaston, who had criticized him severely, died in 1828, and Davy, to whom Faraday owed much but whose growing envy must have been hard to bear, died the following year. Now, for the first time, Faraday felt free to accept responsibilities in the Royal Society, serving on its Council from 1828 to 1831. In 1829 he delivered the prestigious Bakerian Lecture to the society, and in 1832 he delivered a second Bakerian Lecture and received the high honor of its Copley Medal for distinguished scientific research.

In addition to the delivery of his second Bakerian Lecture, 1832 also saw publication of Faraday's paper on "acoustical figures," in which patterns were produced in a fine powder placed on a vibrating plate. Faraday showed these figures, discovered by the German physicist E. F. F.

Chladni, to depend not only on the acoustic vibration but also on the surrounding medium, air or water, for example. The paper was a masterpiece of scientific precision, demonstrating in its author a new confidence and scientific maturity.

Faraday's life with Sarah was equally satisfying. Their happiness endured despite the fact that the marriage was childless, and the couple was devoted to children. The Director's rooms in the Royal Institution often rang with youthful laughter as nephews and nieces came to visit. Two of Sarah's nieces, Jane Barnard and Margery Ann Reid, eventually lived with them for some years, almost as adopted daughters, and Faraday is said to have preferred the company of women to men. Other Sandemanian families visited, and Michael was never more at ease than when romping with children or cavorting with them on his velocipede around the semi-circular corridor surrounding the Theatre downstairs.

At home in his private sanctum Faraday could relax in perfect contentment and welcome the extended family of the Sandemanian faith, for there was much intermarriage, often with two lines doubly linked (as had been the case with Faradays and Hastwells). Michael Faraday's younger sister Margaret had married Sarah's brother John, and several of the Barnards married into the Newcastle Sandemanian family of Reid. Michael's older siblings Robert and Elizabeth also married members of their London congregation.

From their private rooms Michael and Sarah would go to spend most of Sunday at their church, the communion service ("Love Feast") being sandwiched between two other services for teaching and prayer, each often lasting for three hours. After such a spiritual marathon there would be time for family reunions, and a further gathering would take place on Wednesday evenings. During the week Michael Faraday would sometimes get out to visit other Sandemanians, especially those in need. This became more of a duty after his admission as deacon (1832) and elder

(1840), and he gradually became involved in preaching in Sandemanian meetings in London and much further afield.

In the laboratory, although he continued to pursue some research in chemistry in the early 1830s, Faraday returned to the field of electromagnetism, which he had largely abandoned after his initial discoveries 10 years before. There could have been many reasons why Faraday failed to build immediately on his triumphs of the 1820s. He had other priorities, including his chemistry research and the demands of his marriage and responsibilities in the Sandemanian church.

But the primary reason was probably his ambivalent attitude toward André-Marie Ampère's electromagnetic theory. He respected many of the French scientist's ideas, but he could not regard magnetism as a side effect of electric current, as Ampère did. Rather, Faraday thought that a circular force that propelled a magnet around it surrounded a

André-Marie Ampère was a French mathematician/physicist who discovered laws relating to the passage of an electric current down a wire and gave his name to the unit of electric current, the ampere.

wire conveying an electric current. He had a much more symmetrical view of electricity and magnetism, regarding neither as more important than the other. Having produced magnetic effects by an electric current, he did express the desire to "convert magnetism into electricity," but the rather messy state of electromagnetic theory may have deterred him at that time.

But during the 1820s, several advances in electromagnetism were achieved by others, including French astronomer/physicist François Arago and English inventor and bootmaker William Sturgeon. Arago had discovered that if an electrified wire is wound into a coil, a steel rod inserted into the coil becomes magnetized. He also had conducted experiments showing the curious behavior of a compass needle when a flat copper disk was mounted horizontally beneath it. Usually, when a compass is moved, it takes a little while for its needle to come to rest—sometimes oscillating 100 or more times—but the presence of the disk reduced the oscillations to a very small number. Copper is a non-magnetic metal, and yet it was having the effect of a conducting wire on the needle.

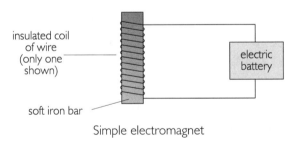

insulated coil of wire (only one shown)

electric battery

soft iron bar

Simple electromagnet

William Sturgeon had invented the electromagnet. He carefully wound a coil of bare copper wire around a piece of soft iron, bent into a horseshoe shape and covered with a layer of insulating varnish. When a current was passed through the wire Sturgeon discovered that the iron became magnetized, and could lift an iron weight of 4 kg. When the current was switched off, the magnetism disappeared and the weight dropped. It is sad to say that Faraday passed over in complete silence the legitimate claims of Sturgeon for the invention of the electromagnet and other important discoveries in electromagnetism. Clearly in this case he did not give credit where that was plainly due. Did he see in the humble bootmaker a more serious rival than the famous Wollaston?

Curiosities such as this were enough to reawaken Faraday's interest in electromagnetism, and he began a key experiment in August 1831 that led to one of the greatest discoveries of his life. He set up a simple apparatus: Two separate wires were coiled around a soft iron ring about 6 inches in external diameter. One of these wires was linked at each end to a battery, while the ends of the other were joined together; however, at one point in the circuit a pivoted magnetized needle was placed underneath, and parallel to, a short length of the wire. When the circuit containing the battery was either completed or broken, the needle near the other circuit twitched and then settled down. It therefore followed that a change in the electric current in the first circuit affected the magnetism of the iron ring. That fact was already well known; what was new, however, was the change in the second circuit. If the needle moved, an electric current must have flowed through the wire above it. In that case, not only did electricity produce a magnetic effect, but also magnetism had produced electricity.

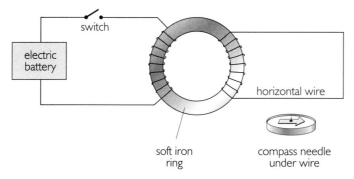

switch
electric battery
horizontal wire
soft iron ring
compass needle under wire

This was the first documented case of electromagnetic induction, though Faraday did not as yet commit himself in writing to that claim. He continued to conduct experiments over the next day or two, then took a three-week break, after which he returned to the problem with renewed energy.

On September 24, Faraday made a triangular arrangement consisting of two permanent bar magnets and a short rod of soft iron linking the north pole of one magnet and the south pole of the other. A coil of wire round the soft iron rod, with its ends joined together, was placed near a magnetized needle as before. When either permanent magnet was moved, the needle registered the passage of a current in the wire above it. Here, then, was evidence of an electric current being created by a mere alteration in the position of a magnet. No use of another electric circuit was required. Electricity was obtained from magnetism alone.

A few days later, he replaced the iron rod with a wooden one. This had very little effect on the magnetized needle. Reverting to his first experiment with an iron ring, he showed that if a small gap interrupted the second circuit, an electric spark jumped across the gap if the iron ring was magnetized. On October 17, he wrapped a coil of wire around a paper cylinder, and connected its ends as usual. When he inserted a magnet into the cylinder, the needle gave a sharp deflection, as though there were a wave of electricity. Other experiments convinced him that magnetism could indeed generate an electric current, and that the metal iron was especially important in such experiments.

When either magnet is moved (as in the dotted lines) the magnetized needle registered a deflection, showing passage of a current in the wire above and demonstrating electricity from magnetism.

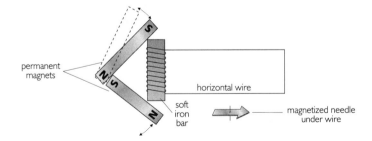

It is important to note that thus far Faraday had not succeeded in obtaining anything like a *continuous* electric current. However, within a few days he hit upon a possible method. He proposed to rotate a copper disk (like the one Arago used) between the poles of a magnet and see if a current could be detected in a circuit connected to the disk. After a few disappointments he made a simple arrangement with one end of the circuit connected to the brass axle on which the disk rotated, and the other touching the edge of the moving wheel. In Faraday's own words, he had obtained "production of a permanent current of electricity by ordinary magnets." He had invented the dynamo.

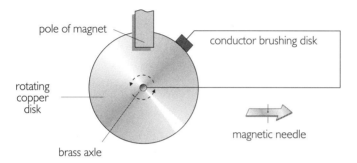

pole of magnet

conductor brushing disk

rotating copper disk

brass axle

magnetic needle

With little fuss the result was reported to the Royal Society in November. Faraday confessed in his diary that the conversion of magnetism into electricity did not really surprise him. If that is so, the closing months of 1831 represented the fulfillment of a 10-year-old dream.

Faraday was careful not to go beyond the experimental facts in his published papers, but an idea that had been slowly maturing in his mind underlay much of his work. This idea was the notion of an "electrotonic state," a state of tension or strain induced in a wire by the passage of an electric current. As soon as electricity flows, the electrotonic state is set up, and this tension causes a magnetized needle to deflect. When the current ceases, the needle deflects in the opposite direction. Thus instead of having a fluid of electricity flowing down a wire, there is a wave of strain moving down it, from one particle to the next. The problem was that no experimental evidence could be obtained for this electrotonic state. Nevertheless it remained a guiding principle in Faraday's mind for many years to come.

These discoveries also marked the beginning of much new electrical research for Faraday, and the start of a new electrical age for civilization. Out of these discoveries emerged the modern dynamo and the vast electrical industry built upon it, although this Faraday could not foresee. Shortly after the results were publicized, British Prime Minister Sir Robert Peel visited the Royal Institution. He asked Faraday what was the use of his new electrical discovery, to which Faraday replied, "I know not, but I wager one day your government will tax it." He was right, of course.

By the end of 1831, Faraday had invented a novelty that could give a continuous electric current, like a battery but using a moving disk in a magnetic field. He was rightly proud of his primitive dynamo, so he was understandably annoyed when the editor of a journal called the *Literary Gazette* announced early in 1832 that Faraday had been beaten by two physicists working in Italy. In fact these two Italians, Leopoldo Nobili and Vicenzo Antinori, had repeated some of Faraday's experiments, having read of them in some garbled accounts then circulating in Paris, but had made full acknowledgment to the source. The careless editor received a very sharp letter from Faraday, confessing, "I have never been more annoyed about any paper than the present [one]." The full publication of Faraday's report to the Royal Society in its *Philosophical Transactions* and of his own notes appended to a translation of the Italians' paper in the *Philosophical Magazine* settled the matter. However, it disclosed a rarely seen side of Faraday's character, namely his sensitivity to his rights in questions of priority and ownership of his work. As Tyndall asserted, "Underneath his sweetness and gentleness was the heat of a volcano," although that heat was nearly always under control.

Faraday was severely rattled by this charge of copying the work of others, so reminiscent of the earlier accusations of Wollaston and Davy. He continued his electrical research, but the reappearance of this controversy may have prompted him to avoid premature leaks of his findings that could damage his claims to originality.

Meanwhile, another fundamental question faced Faraday. For many years, electric effects had been obtainable from a variety of different sources. The oldest of all was static electricity, obtained equally well by the discharge of lightning or by rubbing hair or silk with such materials as ebony, which caused tiny sparks to be seen or heard. Also, it had long been known that certain animals could repel attackers by administering what looked like an electric shock. Since the mid-18th century, it had been known that when sulfur or resins were heated on an insulated dish, some kind of electrification took place; it was later called thermoelectricity. Another kind had appeared in 1800, when Alessandro Volta piled alternating disks of copper, zinc, and damp paper to give rise to a continuous current: Volta's pile was in fact the first electric battery. This electrification was called voltaic electricity, after its discoverer. And Faraday himself had demonstrated the existence of yet another kind, magneto-electricity.

Static electricity was often detected by its ability to cause gold leaves of an electroscope to diverge and was also known to give heat as well as sparks. Many investigators minutely studied voltaic electricity from the year of its announcement, and it showed some of the same effects, as well as another discovered in 1800 by the author William Nicholson and the London surgeon Anthony Carlisle: its ability to decompose solutions of many chemicals, which became known as electrolysis.

For Faraday, the interesting question was whether all these forms of electricity were in reality the same. By 1832 he had demonstrated that this was the case by testing the general effects (such as magnetism or chemical decomposition) of electricity from different sources.

Thus, out of the tiny laboratory in Albemarle Street

came conclusions that were hugely important for the study of electricity, now united into a single new science. Not only was electrical science getting a new unity, but physics and chemistry were to join in yet another new science: electrochemistry.

Faraday had not only studied the general effects of electricity from different sources. He also studied the effects of discharging the same quantities of static and voltaic electricity through a galvanometer, an instrument for measuring the passage of an electric current by the deflection of a needle. He got exactly the same result whatever the intensity (or, in other words, the voltage) of the electricity. In fact he was lucky: An ordinary galvanometer measures not current amount but current flow, but Faraday happened to use a special instrument known as a ballistic galvanometer, which does respond to very small current changes.

But could similar quantitative measurements be made in chemical decompositions? Their extent can be evaluated by measuring, for example, the volume of hydrogen liberated, or the weight of copper deposited. As 1832 drew to a close, Faraday began to work on what he called "electrochemical decomposition." He used a voltammeter to measure the volumes of gases evolved by passage of a current through a solution. He passed a current though a series of cups containing dilute sulfuric acid, but with all kinds of variations in the kinds of conductors leading the current into and out of the solutions. The result was much as he had expected: namely, the extent of electrochemical action depended solely on the amount of current. He had arrived at what came to be called Faraday's First Law of Electrolysis: *The amount of chemical change produced by passage of an electric current is proportional to the quantity of electricity passed.*

Near the end of 1833, Faraday began experimenting with a wide variety of substances dissolved in water in his voltammeters. He rapidly reached another conclusion, known as Faraday's Second Law of Electrolysis: *The amount*

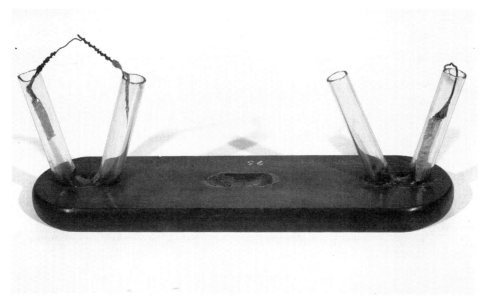

of decomposition by a given amount of electricity depends also on the chemical equivalent of the substance deposited or liberated, a chemical equivalent being the weight that would displace or combine one unit weight of hydrogen; for example, the number of grams of zinc that will displace one gram of hydrogen. Today, the amount of electricity necessary to liberate one chemical equivalent (e.g., 1 gram of hydrogen) is known as the *faraday*. These two laws form the quantitative basis of the science of electrochemistry.

Faraday's theoretical explanations of electrolysis have long been superseded. He thought that the current produced a breakdown of neutral particles into charged particles he called "ions," which travel to the oppositely charged conductor and are then discharged. Electrolysis seemed to be something for which his earlier electrotonic notions might offer an appropriate explanation. However, the absence of experimental evidence after much searching led him eventually to abandon the electrotonic state for the second time in 1835 "as an experimental result," though he still clung to it as a hypothesis. Faraday never solved this problem, although his work eventually led James Clerk Maxwell to figure out

Faraday made or used this equipment in his studies of the chemical effects of an electric current. He placed the solutions to be electrolyzed in the V-shaped glass vessels.

how to apply field theory to magnetism and electricity. Many years later, Albert Einstein took these concepts still further, leading to the theory of a unified field and general relativity.

Electrochemical science also owes to Faraday many terms that are now taken for granted, including *electrolysis,* the process of decomposing a chemical solution by means of electricity; *electrolyte,* the substance in a solution being decomposed; *electrode,* the conductor by which the current enters or leaves the solution; *cathode,* where the current leaves (the negative electrode); *anode,* where the current enters (the positive electrode); *ion,* the charged particle in the solution; *cation,* the ion that is discharged at the cathode; and *anion,* the ion that is discharged at the anode.

The first two terms were probably invented by a friend of Faraday's, Dr. Whitlock Nicholl, and the rest were devised by the mathematician William Whewell, Master of Trinity College, Cambridge (who also invented the word "scientist"). But although Faraday did not originate the terms, he popularized them, introducing them in a paper he read in a lecture in early 1834 and published in the *Philosophical Transactions* shortly afterward.

True to his kaleidoscopic mind, Faraday kept various projects in motion while achieving these advances in electrochemical science. In 1833 he discovered that platinum could be used to catalyze the reaction between hydrogen and oxygen gases to form water. He rightly concluded that this was because the gases were absorbed on to the surface of the metal (which was also susceptible to poisoning by many impurities). On the same theme of metal surfaces he concluded that when iron is rendered "passive," or unreactive, by nitric acid the cause is probably protection by an invisibly thin coat of iron oxide. Other studies ranged from the action of gunpowder on lead to experiments on sodium sulphate, on raw rubber (caoutchouc), and on a new liquid disinfectant containing chlorine.

A far more enduring venture in the large-scale application of science came with Faraday's appointment in 1836 as scientific adviser to Trinity House, the body responsible for all the lighthouses around the coast of England and Wales. He retained this post until 1865. It involved all kinds of duties, including giving advice on ventilation, fog signals, lens manufacture, heating oils, and the merits of the new electric lighting. Faraday sought to make lighthouses more efficient in the fuel they consumed and in the light they produced. His work for Trinity House involved extensive travel, often at some inconvenience. The following account is quite typical; the date was February 1860, and the writer was by then 69 years old:

> I went to Dover last Monday (the 13th instant); was caught in a snow storm between Ashford and Dover and nearly blocked up in the train; could not go to the lighthouse that night; and finding, next day, that the roads on the downs were snowed up, returned to London. On Friday I again went to Dover and proceeded by a fly that night, hoping to find the roads clear of snow; they were still blocked up towards the lighthouse, but by climbing over hedges, walls and fields, I succeeded in getting there and making the necessary inquiries and observations.

It would be easy to assume that Faraday's considerable consulting work, including the Trinity House position, was motivated by a desire to augment his earnings. Certainly he did not think the Royal Institution at all generous in his early days, and from £57 in 1813 his annual salary increased to only £300 in 1853.

By the 1830s Faraday's annual lecture fees came to about £100, and from 1835 on, the Crown granted him a civil list pension of £300. All told, his estimated income was £1,000 a year, maybe up to $100,000 in today's values. The question has been raised as to how far someone as unworldly as Faraday could be happy eventually to receive such a generous income. It is true that Faraday felt underpaid, particularly considering all of his significant accomplishments, although this may have been because the Royal Institution was going through one of its recurrent financial crises. Nevertheless, he clearly felt he deserved adequate payment, and this did not contradict anything the Sandemanian faith, or indeed the Bible, actually taught.

Faraday, as a Sandemanian, was committed to a biblical view of wealth which included such injunctions as "Ye cannot serve God and mammon [worldly values]" (Matthew 6:24) and "Seek ye first the Kingdom of God" (Matthew 6:33). In Faraday's own Bible there were conspicuous vertical lines penciled against the long passage containing the latter verse, as well as many others, including "The love of money is the root of all evil" (1 Timothy 6:10), and "Let your conversation be without covetousness; and be content with such things as ye have; for he hath said, I will never leave thee, nor forsake thee" (Hebrews 13:5).

But Faraday and his fellow believers generally held a balanced view, in which money in itself was a totally unworthy goal, but possessing it was acceptable provided it was acquired honestly and used wisely. In keeping with this philosophy, Faraday often made substantial donations to charity and provided well for his dependents, although we do as yet not know the nature or full extent of his giving.

The physicist John Tyndall, one of Faraday's colleagues at the Royal Institution, asserted that by the 1830s, Faraday's external income had rapidly dwindled to nothing, and in later years he did not even accept his salary of an extra £200 for his services to Trinity House. It has been said that he could have earned £5,000 per year after 1832 had he so wished. And Faraday never patented any of his inventions. All of these facts paint a consistent picture of a man who paid little attention to worldly wealth.

Thus, whenever Faraday decided to work in the world of commerce, it was not for the motive of increasing his wealth. Rather, he sought to pursue natural knowledge for its own sake. In addition, he was deeply concerned to use his science for the material benefit of his fellow citizens, whether they be miners facing explosion hazards, or mariners in a storm-tossed ship peering anxiously for the welcoming and warning beam of one of Britain's many lighthouses. This sentiment was expressed in another verse prominently marked in his Bible: "And let us not be weary in well-doing: for in due season we shall reap, if we faint not" (Galatians 6:9).

Physicist and lawyer William Robert Grove wrote this letter to Faraday in 1842, describing his invention of the "gas battery," or fuel cell.

Electromagnetism: "At Play in the Fields of the Lord"

All the time that Faraday had been pursuing his inquiries into current electricity and into magnetism, he had been dogged by questions as to how the influences, electric or magnetic, were actually transmitted. In Faraday's time there were two fairly common explanations for the transmission of electric and magnetic influences, and he rejected both theories. One was that of material atoms like those proposed by the chemist John Dalton. The other was the old doctrine of action-at-a-distance: namely, that bodies are attracted to one another without any intermediate bodies to pass on the effects. That was one reason why Faraday came to his theory of "fields," which were mechanical agencies to transport energy across a distance. Possibly he was also indebted to some similar ideas proposed by the 18th-century Italian mathematician R. J. Boscovich.

Faraday had concluded that some kind of force must exist even across empty space. He spoke first of "magnetic curves," then of "lines of force," and eventually of a magnetic "field." The lines of force could be elegantly illustrated by the familiar experiment of sprinkling iron filings on a sheet of paper placed over a magnet, and recognition of such lines made his electrotonic state theory superfluous. He reluctantly abandoned it for solid conductors. Faraday went on to suggest that lines of force from the earth's magnetism might be responsible for phenomena like the aurora borealis (more familiarly known as the northern lights), which is visible in the sky near the North Pole and probably caused by electrically charged particles.

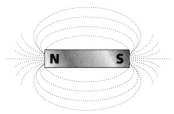

Iron filings are sprinkled onto a piece of paper situated just above a magnet. When the paper is gently tapped, the filings line up along the presumed "lines of force."

In the late 1960s, a document was discovered in the library of the Institution of Electrical Engineers. It was a private memorandum by Faraday that clarified his ideas on atoms and fields. Unlike his published papers, it contains several references to God, one of which wondered whether God could not as easily put "power" round point centers as he could about material nuclei. His belief in an all-powerful God led him to the idea of point centers, and thus of fields around them. Professor Trevor Levere of Toronto, who discovered this document, remarked that these new ideas "fitted in with the world picture imposed by his religion." Thereafter, as one writer put it, "Faraday was, quite literally, at play in the fields of the Lord."

To study further the transmission of electric force, Faraday left current electricity and magnetism and turned to static electricity, since charges of static electricity could be stored in various kinds of condensers. These could be a glass Leyden jar or a hollow brass sphere inside another slightly larger one. None of these condensers, however, was more spectacular than one built to Faraday's specifications in 1835.

It was a wooden-framed cube, each side 12 feet long, covered with wire gauze. Faraday knew that a charge induced on a hollow vessel existed on the outer surface, but he needed to demonstrate that it was only there, and not in the interior. He therefore made a cage large enough for him to enter with his instruments. As he expected, there was no charge and he was unharmed, even when the case was crackling with huge amounts of static electricity. This was the Faraday cage that eventually became part of Faraday's most spectacular lecture-demonstrations in the Lecture Theatre.

On a much smaller scale, in 1837 Faraday took one of the spherical condensers and showed that, by interposing an insulator between the plates, he obtained different amounts of charge depending on the material of the insulator. The question seemed to center on the time it took the electricity to penetrate the insulator (or "dielectric" as it was sometimes called) when attempts were made to charge the plates. He called the measure of the readiness for the dielectric to permit the passage of an electric charge the "specific inductive capacity," now generally known as dielectric constant. In honor of the discoverer, this capacity is now measured in *farads*. No other scientist has ever had two units named after him. Faraday explained the effect in terms of adjacent particles jostling each other in the dielectric, with each one receiving its charge from the one next to it.

Between 1838 and 1840 Faraday's health began to fail. First it was a combination of rheumatism and fatigue, but before long his illness showed itself as fits of giddiness accompanied by loss of short-term memory—the latter affliction being by far the hardest for Faraday to bear. At the end of 1839, he was compelled to take a holiday, and in 1841 he went on an eight-month tour of Switzerland. For the next three or four years he was forced to abandon nearly all attempts at research. He gave a few lectures and discourses during that period, and he also became an elder in the Sandemanian church, but for much of the time he relaxed at the theater, the zoo, or simply at home. Such enforced idleness might be attractive to some people, but it vexed Faraday, for whom work was a delight as well as a duty.

In 1844, the Home Secretary called him to that duty as an expert witness in the case of a mine explosion that claimed the lives of 95 men and boys at Haswell Colliery, County Durham. Faraday and the geologist Charles Lyell were asked to attend the inquest and offer expert advice. To Faraday and Lyell it appeared that the cause of the explosion was ignition of an accumulation of methane gas from a faulty Davy lamp that had collected in a "goaf" (a kind of underground dome). The verdict was accidental death. The mine owners were not held responsible.

Faraday's failure to condemn the exploitation of poor miners by wealthy mine owners, combined with his deep dislike of revolutionary politics, has led some people to believe he was a Tory, preferring the status quo and reluctant to criticize established institutions. Yet this is to ignore the Sandemanian roots of Faraday's belief, which distanced itself from all political systems and was not afraid to criticize that most conspicuous feature of the establishment, the Church of England. No sound Tory would do that. A conservative by inclination in some respects, Faraday was a thorough radical in others, notably in issues concerning church and state.

Also in 1844, for reasons that are far from clear, Faraday and 18 other Sandemanians were "excluded" from the London church. The standard explanation in Faraday's case was that he breached church discipline by accepting an invitation to dine with Queen Victoria one Sunday, when he was expected to be in church. No evidence has been found to support this contention, however, and at any rate it did not explain why the other members were excluded. It is more likely that the cause was a furious argument within the church at the time over whether its elders could make decisions on behalf of the whole church. Faraday, to whom holding power within the church was not a primary interest, probably disagreed with his fellow elders on this matter. Fortunately, the question was settled quickly, and six weeks later Faraday and most of the others were readmitted. The suspension profoundly affected Faraday's spirits, and may well have been partly responsible for another spell of illness that befell him in 1844.

Fortunately, by 1845 Faraday was noticeably better, and he was able to move toward what could be considered his supreme scientific achievement. Having discovered fundamental laws about nonconductors of electricity (dielectrics) in 1836, he turned nearly a decade later to a study of materials that did not appear capable of being magnetized (which included almost everything except iron and one or two other metals). He was encouraged in this direction by correspondence with a young Scottish physicist named William Thomson (later Lord Kelvin, best known for his later development of the absolute temperature scale). Wondering whether light and electricity were in some way related, he had tried to examine the effects of a strong electrical field on plane-polarized light (that is, light whose vibrations are confined to one plane). When such light passes through certain crystals, the plane is rotated through an angle, and this is readily detected. However, Faraday was unable to get a similar effect with the best electrical field available. So he turned to magnetism, using the most powerful electromagnet he could acquire.

He used some of the fine optical glass from his experiments of long ago, since this was known to refract light very strongly. He suspended a piece in the magnetic field and passed a ray of polarized light through the glass. With the relatively small magnets then at his disposal, he got only a slight effect. But on September 18 he began to use a very powerful electromagnet that he had borrowed from the Royal Military Academy at Woolwich. To his delight there was an effect, which triumphantly confirmed his belief that magnetism and light were related. Having worked like a maniac with many different substances, that evening he could write, with masterly understatement, "an excellent day's work."

The rotation of the plane of polarization in a magnetic field is now known as "the Faraday effect." It became the basis of another new science: magneto-optics. He reflected on these results in a letter to his friend Richard Phillips in April 1846, subsequently printed in the *Philosophical Magazine* as an article entitled "Thoughts on Ray Vibrations." John Tyndall considered the paper "one of the most singular speculations that ever emanated from a scientific man." Faraday was coming very close to an explicit announcement that light is a form of electromagnetic radiation, thus uniting optics with magnetism and electricity. This idea influenced James Clerk Maxwell, who discussed it in his "Dynamical Theory of the Electromagnetic Field," a major paper he published in 1864.

Faraday announced his results at the Royal Institution on November 3, 1845, and sent them to the Royal Society on November 6. But something of such moment had happened that he even denied himself the pleasure of attendance at the Royal Society on November 20, when his paper was read on his behalf. Visitors were denied access to the laboratory, and he wrote "I hardly have time for my meals." In fact on November 4 he had discovered yet another new phenomenon of immense importance to science. Using the Woolwich magnet, he had found that materials that were not magnetic were nevertheless moved by the magnetic field. He suspended a small bar of his borosilicate glass between the poles of his great electromagnet and saw that when the current was switched on, the magnet caused the glass to rotate until it settled perpendicular to the magnetic field. In other words, it pointed east-to-west, whereas iron and a few other metals pointed north-to-south. He concluded that it was seeking the weakest points of the magnetic field. Substances that behaved in this manner he called diamagnetic materials, for they settled across the field (the prefix *dia* means "across"). By contrast, paramagnetic materials, such as iron, cobalt and nickel, settled parallel to the magnetic field. He experimented with a great number of diamagnetic materials, including metals, of which bismuth was the most strongly diamagnetic.

Faraday's discovery of diamagnetism caused him so much excitement and nervous strain that he was compelled to take a holiday in Brighton shortly afterward. Even there, however, he could not restrain himself from communicating his results privately to a friend of his, the Swiss physicist Auguste de la Rive. Again a new science bridging the subject areas of magnetism and chemistry sprang from these findings. Known as magnetochemistry, it has proved of great value in determining chemical structures. Even that was not the end of the matter.

Believing that all substances not actually paramagnetic should show diamagnetic behavior, Faraday, on his return to London, resumed his studies in this area with great vigor. No doubt Faraday's belief in the unity of the forces of matter was reinforced by his faith in a Creator who made the whole universe work together in harmony. Therefore, what applied to solids should also apply to liquids and gases. Early results were disappointing, but Faraday seems to have been encouraged by the discovery by the Italian scientist Michele Bancalari in 1847 of diamagnetism in flames (which are, after all, burning gases). Between then and 1851, Faraday repeated many of Bancalari's findings. Not only did he succeed in showing that many common gases were diamagnetic, but he also found, in experiments performed in 1849–50, that oxygen was considerably paramagnetic. He used this surprising result to formulate a theory of the earth's magnetism based on the fact of oxygen's paramagnetism. And it confirmed once again the great interconnectedness of the whole universe scanned by science.

Michael and Sarah Faraday and their niece Jane Barnard in about 1858; at left is Faraday's colleague at the Royal Institution, the physicist John Tyndall.

CHAPTER

10

Waning Years

In spite of his groundbreaking discoveries concerning diamagnetism, the electromagnetic nature of light, and the
paramagnetism of oxygen, Faraday had never fully recovered
from his earlier illness. As mentioned before, the most
annoying symptom of his malady was his tendency to forget
recent events. This presented a great hindrance to scientific
research, which in most cases has to take into account work
that others have done in the recent past. He wrote at one
point, "Want of memory made me give up with many lines
of research which else I should have worked on—and seek
those on which nobody was moving—hence Rotation of
light and diamagnetism."

After this he made frequent references to loss of memory in his letters, though he rarely complained. In 1861 he
made something of a joke about it in a letter to de la Rive:
"If my memory fails—why it causes that I forget *troubles* as
well as pleasure; & the end is I am happy and content."

On a visit to Glasgow two years later, he wrote to
Sarah, sending his love and that of "a great many others
which I cannot call to mind" and adding:

I long to see you, dearest, and to talk over things together, and call to mind all the kindness I have received. My head is full, and my heart also, but my recollection rapidly fails, even as regards the friends that are in the room with me. You will have to resume your old function of being a pillow to my mind, and a rest, a happy-making wife.

Despite these problems, it would be wrong to suppose that the two decades from 1845 were destitute of any scientific interest or achievements by Faraday. Quite the opposite, in fact. Although Faraday's mental powers had begun to fail at an alarmingly early age (he had been only 48 in 1839, when his symptoms first appeared), he continued to work whenever possible, performing his own research, advising others, and promoting the cause of science by word and in print. His work for Trinity House actually increased during these years. Consultant work of this kind requires great scientific skill and persistence and a deep, broad appreciation of what science has done and can do, but not a recollection of the details of every latest advance. In 1852, he worked for the Electric Telegraph Company on the effects of submersion on the insulation of electric cables. In addition, he studied the preservation of ships' timbers and the disinfection of prisons. He maintained much correspondence with many scientists, often in answer to specific queries about scientific applications. For instance, he wrote to British engineer Sir Marc Isambard Brunel about his Thames Tunnel and his attempts to use condensed gas as a locomotive fuel. He also exchanged letters with astronomers such as Sir John Herschel, geologists such as Jean Louis Agassiz, physiologists like Emil du Bois-Reymond, and a large number of chemists and physicists.

Faraday also continued his studies on the effects of pollution on works of art. This occurred not only in the gaslit library of the Athenaeum Club, but anywhere that was touched by the London fogs, called "pea-soupers" because of their yellow tinge caused by the burning of coal. This foul pollution affected the oil paintings in the National Gallery, but Faraday showed that ethanol removed the dirty varnishes that sometimes covered the paintings. At the British Museum, priceless, ancient relics were becoming seriously darkened by London grime. Faraday showed that many statues and objects such as the Elgin Marbles were being penetrated deeply by fine channels caused presumably by the action of sulfuric acid in the atmosphere. Unfortunately, removing the dirt from these hairline channels was an impossible task at that time.

Faraday's concern for the environment was not limited to the air in venerable buildings. In July 1855 he wrote a letter to the *Times,* complaining of the foul pollution of the

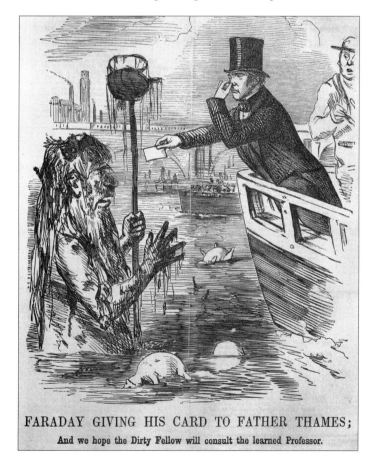

FARADAY GIVING HIS CARD TO FATHER THAMES;

And we hope the Dirty Fellow will consult the learned Professor.

In July 1855, after a boat trip down the Thames, Faraday wrote to the Times *reporting the appalling river pollution. When he dropped a visiting card edgeways into the water, the lower half was invisible before the upper half entered the water. The popular magazine* Punch *commented with a cartoon.*

River Thames, then the source of most of London's drinking-water. He described a trip by steamboat between London and Hungerford Bridges:

> The whole of the river was an opaque pale brown fluid. In order to test the degree of opacity, I tore up some white cards into pieces, moistened them so as to make them sink easily below the surface, and then dropped some of these pieces into the water at every pier the boat came to; before they had sunk an inch below the surface they were indistinguishable, though the sun shone brightly at the time; and when the pieces fell edgeways the lower part was hidden from sight before the upper party was under water . . . . Near the bridges the feculence rolled up in clouds so dense that they were visible at the surface, even in water of this kind. The smell was very bad, and common to the whole of the water; it was the same as that which now comes up from the gully-holes in the streets; the whole river was for the time a real sewer . . .

This letter was especially timely, as it appeared the year after London had suffered a severe epidemic of cholera, one of the worst known water-borne diseases. It was one of the first attempts to bring out into the open the enormous dangers inherent in water pollution; however, many years would pass before science could properly identify the real dangers and learn how to avoid them.

By now Faraday's fame extended far beyond the Royal Institution, the scientific establishment of London, and even the shores of Great Britain. He was elected to membership in nearly 70 learned societies from Boston to Moscow, from Uppsala to Mauritius. Yet he declined many offers, preferring to live simply, and maintained his indifference to worldly wealth. In the late 1850s, he declined to sanction a lucrative publication of his lectures on metals, writing: "I do not desire to give time to them, for money is no temptation to me. In fact I have always loved science more than money; and because my occupation is almost entirely personal, I cannot afford to get rich."

Most remarkably, in 1857 he resisted considerable peer pressure to accept the presidency of the Royal Society, probably the most prestigious scientific office in the world. He told his friend John Tyndall, "If I accepted the honor which the Royal Society desires to confer upon me, I could not answer for the integrity of my intellect for a single year," implying that he would find the work too much. Faraday had little interest in worldly honors and had in fact declined the offer of a knighthood some years before. This was Sandemanian spirituality at its simplest. As he told Tyndall, "I must remain plain Michael Faraday to the last."

Although Faraday never sought favors from Queen Victoria, and rarely attended royal functions unless he had to, he was highly regarded by Prince Albert, who sometimes attended his lectures. It was at Albert's request that, in 1858, Queen Victoria placed at Faraday's disposal one of her houses on the green near Hampton Court, on the Thames to the west of London. Although small by royal

The great men of the Royal Society—Lord Wrottesley, J. P. Gassiot, and W. R. Grove—try unsuccessfully to persuade Michael Faraday (far right) to become their president in 1858.

standards, it was incomparably finer than any house Faraday had yet inhabited, and certainly better than any his family had occupied in Mallerstang. Faraday hesitated to accept the generous offer on account of the probable costs of renovation, but on learning this the queen instructed that all the necessary work should be done at her expense. When Faraday's weakness got worse, she also arranged for all of the living accommodations to be on one level, on the first floor. At first Michael and Sarah Faraday continued to use their existing accommodation at the Royal Institution, but from 1862 the house at Hampton Court became their only home.

As time—and memory—permitted, Faraday frequently continued to engage in his own personal research. From now on, his aim was to test his theories as thoroughly and relentlessly as possible. His manipulative skills seemed unimpaired, as did his extraordinary gift of inventing experiments that could tease out the evidence for or against a particular theory. Faraday's conclusions of the 1830s and 1840s on the problems of electricity and magnetism held up remarkably well against his repeated attempts to undermine them.

He even tried to extend his conquest of the physical world by including gravity in his grand unified scheme. He especially wished to find some way to connect gravity to electricity. To do so, he used the famous Shot Tower on the South Bank of the Thames. Measuring 165 feet high, it was used to drop molten lead which, by the time it reached the bottom, had cooled and separated into small solid spheres of lead shot. Faraday used the tower to drop a large insulated lump of lead whose electrical charge, if any, could be measured before and after it descended. After repeated efforts, Faraday found the experiment gave no detectable changes and concluded that here, at least, there was no experimental link between electricity and gravity. In fact, as we now know, gravitational forces are very different from those encountered in optics, electricity, and magnetism, and Faraday's conclusions were right.

He submitted the results of this latest experiment to *Philosophical Transactions* in 1860 but was advised to withdraw by the Cambridge physicist George Stokes, who was also secretary of the Royal Society. Stokes's reason, he said, was that Faraday was merely reporting a negative result, and that was unworthy of such an eminent journal unless it contradicted a widely held belief. Stokes did not share Faraday's vision of a unified physics and so regarded the result as fairly unimportant. Even though he shared much of Faraday's evangelical religion, Stokes did not draw from it the same conclusions about nature. That was the last paper Faraday submitted for publication. Its effective rejection indicates just how far he was removed from conventional physics by this time.

Faraday still devoted some time and energy to further work, however. In 1862 he attempted to discover if an electromagnetic field would affect the lines in a spectrum emitted by sodium and other metals that were heated in a flame. When the poles of a powerful electromagnet were placed around the flame, and the electric current was allowed to flow, Faraday could detect no change whatever in the position or size of the spectral lines. Had he done so, it would have been another new link between magnetism and light. In fact a Dutch physicist, Pieter Zeeman, stimulated by Faraday's negative result, was more successful 35 years later, using a much more powerful magnet and better spectroscopic apparatus. He found that the lines of the spectrum were slightly widened by the application of the magnetic field, thus leading to the measurement of the mass of an electron and the extension of the quantum theory. If better equipment had been available in 1862, Faraday could well have discovered the Zeeman effect.

Nevertheless, by the 1860s, it was clear that Faraday, now into his 70s, would have to face retirement with all the losses that inevitably meant. First to go were his Christmas Lectures; he gave his final one in 1861. He delivered his last Friday night discourse, on the gas furnaces of the German engineer Charles William Siemens, on June 20, 1862, a few weeks after making the final entry in his laboratory notebook. Two years later, he resigned from his position as elder in the Sandemanian church, and the next year, in 1865, he stepped down from the position of superintendent of the house at the Royal Institution and severed his long connection with Trinity House. For the remaining two years of his life he was largely confined to his chair at home, and those who came to see him were impressed as much by his serenity as his withdrawal from the world of science he had served so long.

By now Michael Faraday had been at work in his laboratory for nearly half a century. During that time he had explored hundreds of avenues in the growing sciences of electricity and magnetism—a lone pioneer in uncharted territory. Often success eluded him, but from time to time the results came so thick and fast that he eventually had to take a period of enforced rest. New sciences, such as electromagnetism, magneto-optics, and diamagnetism, emerged from his work, while the field of electrochemistry took giant strides forward under his watch. From his discoveries came the dynamo and electric motor. And beneath the spectacular discoveries, there lay a science unified as never before, ready to be taken to new depths of understanding by those who followed Faraday.

In addition, Faraday emerged as one of Britain's very best communicators of science, whose writings and Royal Institution lectures brought science to new heights of popularity. Year in and year out, he filled the famous Lecture Theatre with astonishing performances of scientific experiments, accompanied by commentaries that kept the audience spellbound. All the while, Faraday turned his attentions to what he saw as another social duty: to apply science to the practical affairs of his fellow citizens by advising on the production of metals, glass, and many other materials, and on the state and operation of Britain's lighthouses. But the time was fast approaching for all these activities to come to an end.

One short letter he wrote in 1861 to de la Rive discloses something of the inner strength he drew from his Christian faith as the world he had known for so long was beginning to collapse all around him:

> Such peace is alone in the gift of God; and as it is He who gives it why should we be afraid? His unspeakable gift in His beloved Son is the ground of no doubtful hope.

In that year Charles Darwin published his book *The Origin of Species,* which many have seen as undermining such a confident faith. The remarkable thing is that Faraday says nothing about evolution that implies any kind of unresolvable problem. Though by now his physical condition was deteriorating, he could think clearly for much of the time and express himself eloquently where that was necessary. His silence on Darwin's work is highly significant. Like many physical scientists, he may have dismissed evolution as "only a theory." More probably his faith was so strong that nothing, even in science, could shake it.

As the end approached, his friends, family, and his medical caretakers alike testified to his quiet confidence. In his times of lucidity, he spoke of his comfort in Christ, and dwelled on such passages as the 23rd ("The Lord is my shepherd; I shall not want...") and 46th ("God is our refuge and strength...") Psalms. Then, on August 25, 1867, while sitting quietly in his study chair, he died.

Four days later, his funeral took place at Highgate Cemetery in north London, attended only by close family and a few personal friends. At his request, there was neither ceremony nor pomp. (In 1991, a formal service was held at Westminster Abbey to celebrate the 200th anniversary of his birth; doubtless this would have appalled him.) As was Sandemanian custom, his body was laid to rest in soil that was not "consecrated" by ecclesiastical ceremony, without a religious service (for none was enjoined in Scripture), and in perfect silence. At the head of the grave a simple stone carries the words:

Michael Faraday
Born 22 September 1791
Died 25 August 1867

So passed away "the greatest experimental philosopher the world has ever seen" (in the words of Tyndall), someone who changed the face of modern science, and therefore of society itself. He has been described by Maxwell as "the father of the enlarged science of electromagnetism" and by Lord Kelvin as "the inspiring influence of my early love of electricity." He has been the subject of more biographies than even Newton and Einstein.

Whatever else may have contributed to his towering achievements, there is no doubt that Faraday's science owed a great deal to his religion. Even the agnostic Tyndall recognized that "his religious feeling & his philosophy could not be kept apart." Many examples of this have already been given: his conviction of a unity in the natural world, his preference for point-centers of force rather than Daltonian atoms, a theologically inspired reverence for nature, and his sheer joy and determination to understand the works of the Creator. When he famously announced in 1844 that "there is no 'philosophy' in my religion," he did not mean that there was no connection at all between scientific and religious truth. Rather, he was saying that scientific knowledge (what he called "philosophy") could neither illuminate religion nor lead men to God. His lecturing skills, his dislike of "systems," and his desire to benefit his fellow citizens through science all had close parallels in the Sandemanian faith and practice. His faith gave meaning, purpose, and shape to his whole life, scientific and otherwise.

Although Michael Faraday was in a class of his own where science was concerned—a giant among pygmies—he was typical of many gifted scientists in his synthesis of science and Christianity, in his strong confidence in the authority of Scripture, and in his simple faith in Christ. For them, and for him, the task of scientific exploration was not only exciting and satisfying. In a very real sense it was a Christian vocation. Nothing less than this can enable us to understand the life and achievements of Michael Faraday.

CHRONOLOGY

1791
Michael Faraday born, London

1804
Begins work with G. Riebau, bookbinder and bookseller

1812
Hears Humphry Davy speak at the Royal Institution

1813
Appointed assistant at the Royal Institution

1813–15
Takes a scientific tour of Europe with Sir Humphry Davy

1815
Becomes assistant and superintendent of apparatus at the Royal Institution

1815–16
Works with Davy on the miners' safety lamp

1821
Marries Sarah Barnard; joins Sandemanian church; first experiments on electromagnetic rotation

1821–22
Discovers two chlorides of carbon

1823–24
Achieves liquefaction of gases

1825
Discovers benzene and isobutylene

1829
Accepts part-time professorship at Royal Military Academy, Woolwich

1831
Discovers electromagnetic induction

1833
Discovers "Faraday's laws" of electrolysis

1836
Appointed scientific Adviser to Trinity House; works on electrostatics and dielectrics

1840
Appointed elder of Sandemanian church

1845
Studies diamagnetism and paramagnetism, as well as magneto-optics

1849
Attempts to unite gravity and electricity

1858
Given house at Hampton Court by Queen Victoria

1861
Resigns professorship at Royal Institution

1862
Studies effects of magnetic fields on spectral lines

1867
Dies at Hampton Court home

Books by Michael Faraday

Faraday, Michael. *Chemical Manipulation: Being Instructions to Students in Chemistry, on the Methods of Performing Experiments of Demonstration or of Research, with Accuracy and Success.* Ed. J. K. Mitchell. Philadelphia: Carey and Lea, 1831.

_____. *The Correspondence of Michael Faraday,* 6 vols. Ed. Frank A. J. L. James. London: Institution of Electrical Engineers, 1991.

_____. *Course of Six Lectures on the Chemical History of a Candle.* Chicago: Chicago Review Press, 1988.

_____. *Diary,* 8 vols. Ed. T. Martin. London: Bell, 1932–36.

_____. *Experimental Researches in Electricity,* 3 vols. New York: Dover, 1965.

_____. *Experimental Researches in Chemistry and Physics.* New York: Taylor & Francis, 1991.

Books about Michael Faraday

Agassi, Joseph. *Faraday as a Natural Philosopher.* Chicago: University of Chicago Press, 1971.

Appleyard, Rollo. *A Tribute to Michael Faraday.* London: Constable, 1931.

Ashcroft, E. W. *Faraday.* London: British Electrical & Allied Manufacturers Association, 1931.

Cantor, Geoffrey. *Michael Faraday: Sandemanian and Scientist: A Study of Science and Religion in the 19th Century.* New York: St. Martin's Press, 1991.

_____, David Gooding, and Frank A. J. L. James. *Faraday.* London: Macmillan, 1991.

Crowther, J. G. *British Scientists of the 19th Century.* London: Routledge & Kegan Paul, 1962.

Gladstone, John H. *Michael Faraday.* London: Macmillan, 1872.

Gooding David, and Frank A. J. L. James, eds. *Faraday Rediscovered: Essays on the Life and Work of Michael Faraday, 1791–1867.* New York: Stockton Press, 1985.

Gunston, David. *Michael Faraday: Father of Electricity.* London: Weidenfeld & Nicholson, 1962.

Jeffreys, Alan E., ed. *Michael Faraday: A List of His Lectures and Published Writings.* New York: Academic Press, 1961.

Jerrold, Walter C. *Michael Faraday: Man of Science.* London: S. W. Partridge, 1891.

Jones, H. Bence. *The Life and Letters of Faraday.* London: Longmans, 1870.

Kendall, James. *Great Discoveries by Young Chemists.* New York: Nelson, 1953.

Riley, James F. *The Hammer and the Anvil: A Background to Michael Faraday.* Clapham, England: Dalesman Publishing, 1954.

Thomas, John Meurig. *Michael Faraday and the Royal Institution.* Philadelphia: A. Hilger, 1991.

Thompson, Sylvanus P. *Michael Faraday: His Life and Work.* New York: Cassell, 1901.

Tyndall, John. *Faraday as a Discoverer.* London: Longmans, 1868.

Williams, L. Pearce. *Michael Faraday, A Biography.* New York: Basic Books, 1965.

_____, ed. *The Selected Correspondence of Michael Faraday,* 2 vols. Cambridge: Cambridge University Press, 1971.

Books about the Royal Institution

Berman, Morris. *Social Change and Scientific Organization: The Royal Institution, 1799–1844.* Ithaca: Cornell University Press, 1978.

Caroe, Gwendy. *The Royal Institution: An Informal History.* London: Murray, 1985.

Greenaway, Frank, ed. *Archives of the Royal Institution.* London: Scholar Press, 1971–74.

Jones, H. Bence. *The Royal Institution: Its Founder and Its First Professors.* London: Longmans, 1870.

Martin, Thomas. *The Royal Institution.* New York: Longmans, Green, 1948.

A Keen Mind, p. 13: In Michael Faraday, *The Correspondence of Michael Faraday,* 6 vols. Ed. Frank A. J. L. James. London: Institution of Electrical Engineers, 1991.

The Chemical History of a Candle, pp. 76–77: In Michael Faraday, *A Course of Six Lectures, on the Chemical History of a Candle; to Which Is Added a Lecture on Platinum.* Ed. W. Crookes. London: Griffin, 1861.

Colin Russell is a chemist as well as Emeritus and Visiting Research Professor at the Open University in the department of history of science and technology, which he founded in 1970. He has done many TV and radio broadcasts and has written extensively on the history of the physical sciences. His books include *Edward Frankland: Chemistry, Controversy and Conspiracy in Victorian England,* a major biography of the leading British chemist. In 1990 the American Chemical Society awarded him the Dexter Award for outstanding contributions to the history of chemistry.

Owen Gingerich is Professor of Astronomy and of the History of Science at the Harvard-Smithsonian Center for Astrophysics in Cambridge, Massachusetts. The author of more than 400 articles and reviews, he has also written *The Great Copernicus Chase and Other Adventures in Astronomical History* and *The Eye of Heaven: Ptolomy, Copernicus, Kepler.*